PRAYER AND
WORSHIP

OTHER RENOVARÉ RESOURCES

Connecting with God
by Lynda L. Graybeal and Julia L. Roller

Devotional Classics
co-edited by Richard J. Foster and James Bryan Smith

Embracing the Love of God
by James Bryan Smith

Learning from Jesus
by Lynda L. Graybeal and Julia L. Roller

The Renovaré Spiritual Formation Bible
edited by Richard J. Foster and others

Songs for Renewal
by Janet Lindeblad Janzen with Richard J. Foster

Spiritual Classics
co-edited by Richard J. Foster and Emilie Griffin

A Spiritual Formation Journal
created by Jana Rea with Richard J. Foster

A Spiritual Formation Workbook
by James Bryan Smith with Lynda L. Graybeal

Streams of Living Water
by Richard J. Foster

Wilderness Time
by Emilie Griffin

OTHER BOOKS
BY RICHARD J. FOSTER

Celebrating the Disciplines
with Kathryn A. Helmers

Celebration of Discipline

The Challenge of the Disciplined Life

Freedom of Simplicity

Prayer: Finding the Heart's True Home

Prayers from the Heart

Richard J. Foster's Study Guide for Celebration of Discipline

Seeking the Kingdom

PRAYER AND
WORSHIP

A SPIRITUAL FORMATION GUIDE

A RENOVARÉ RESOURCE

FOR INDIVIDUALS AND GROUPS

Introduction by Richard J. Foster

Lynda L. Graybeal and Julia L. Roller

HarperOne
A Division of HarperCollinsPublishers

HarperOne

For information about RENOVARÉ write to RENOVARÉ, 8 Inverness Dr East, Suite 102, Englewood, CO 80112-5624 USA or log on to the Web site http://www.renovare.org.

HarperCollins books may be purchased for educational, business, or sales promotional use. For information please write: Special Markets Department, HarperCollins Publishers, 10 East 53rd Street, New York, NY 10022.

HarperCollins Web site: http://www.harpercollins.com

HarperCollins®, ♣®, and HarperOne™ are trademarks of HarperCollins Publishers.

FIRST EDITION
Designed by Sharon VanLoozenoord

Library of Congress Cataloging-in-Publication Data is available.

ISBN: 978-0-06-084125-6
ISBN-10: 0-06-084125-7

07 08 09 10 11 RRD (H) 10 9 8 7 6 5 4 3 2 1

CONTENTS

INTRODUCTION

For five years I engaged in what is bound to be my life's richest adventure of biblical work. Five of us (in time to be called general editors) were wrestling with the whole of Scripture through the lens of spiritual formation, seeing what we could learn and how we could be formed and conformed and transformed ever more deeply in the subterranean chambers of the soul. That project eventually came into published form as *The Renovaré Spiritual Formation Bible*.

How do I describe to you the excitement of those early days? To be sure, it was genuine work, for the intensity of labor was exhausting, but it was so much more than "work." It was the thrill of creative ideas flying fast and furious, of dynamic insights crammed one upon another. In those chaotic sessions I often felt like I was astride a wild stallion at full gallop, gripping the mane for dear life.

But it wasn't just the excitement of new concepts emerging out of the wealth of pooled intellectual capital. No, it was the sense of awe before the majesty of Scripture, of being drawn in toward the Divine Center, of holy stillness, of quiet worship and whispered promptings. And prayers—morning prayers and evening prayers and days soaked in prayerful sharing over the sacred text. Oh yes, and laughter. Deep, side-splitting belly laughter. Holy hilarity I guess you could call it.

The experience was joyfully creative and soul-expanding. We knew we were onto something big—big ideas with huge consequences for the hearts and minds of precious people.

At some point in this dynamic process we began to ask if a way could be found to help those who would read this *Renovaré Bible* to experience something of the excitement and adventure we had in first hammering out the concepts of the "Immanuel Principle" and the "with-God life." Could others discover for themselves how the "with-God" framework illuminates God's purposes in history? How over many centuries and through multiple human authors, God has so superintended the development of the Bible that it speaks to us about real life (*zoë*) and teaches us how to live "with God" through the vicissitudes of human experience? How the aim of God in history is the creation of an all-inclusive community of loving persons, with God himself included in this community as its prime sustainer and most glorious inhabitant? How the unity of the Bible is discovered in the lived community reality of this *zoë* life under God and with God and through the power of God?

And so these spiritual formation guides were born. Together they will take us on a journey through the entire panorama of Scripture. Through these spiritual formation guides, we will discover how the Old Testament depicts God's pursuit of loving relationship with his chosen people, Israel, and how through Israel all the peoples of the earth are to be blessed. We see this "pursuit of loving relationship" carried on through the lives of the patriarchs, the history of the Israelites in their exodus from slavery and their entrance into the Promised Land, in the forming and then the disintegration of tribe and nation. Then, the New Testament depicts the story of God's fulfillment of "loving relationship" with a people who become God's own through their identity in Jesus Christ: "God's household, having been built upon the foundation of the apostles and prophets, Christ Jesus Himself being the corner *stone,* in whom the whole building, being fitted together, is growing into a holy temple in the Lord; in whom you also are being built together into a dwelling of God in the Spirit" (Eph 2:19–22, NASB).

As the Bible closes, it opens a window onto the fulfillment of God's purposes for humanity beyond human history: "Now the dwelling of God is with human beings, and he will live with them. They will be his people, and God himself will be with them and be their God" (Rev 21:3, NIVI).

Thus, we will discover that the Immanuel Principle is, after all, a cosmic principle that God has used all along in creation and redemption. It alone serves to guide human life aright on earth now and even illuminates the future of the universe. Of course, the few examples I have shared here hardly touch the surface of the great river of life that flows from God through Scripture and into the thirsty wastelands of the human soul. "Let anyone who is thirsty come to me [Jesus] and drink. Whoever believes in me, as the Scripture has said, will have streams of living water flowing from within" (John 7:37–38, NIVI).

This study guide, therefore, has been created to help each of us enter into the story of the Bible so as to see our own story, our own journey in the great cosmic drama of divine-human relationship. May you, may I, choose to surrender freely to this river of life, receiving and helping others to receive this Life, this *Zoë,* as our own.

Richard J. Foster

HOW TO USE THIS GUIDE

This book is dedicated to nurturing spiritual formation through the study of Scripture. Devotional excerpts from the writings of ancient and contemporary Christians; questions for reflection; and exercises centered around Spiritual Disciplines, such as study, prayer, solitude, meditation, and silence; supplement and illumine the biblical text. This book is not intended to be read passively; it requires the interactive participation of you the reader. To engage with the texts we have chosen and to do the exercises we have set out here will require time and dedication beyond mere reading of the guide. We hope you will accept this challenge!

Whether you are using the guide as an individual or as a group, we recommend that you begin by reading "The With-God Life" and becoming familiar with the accompanying chart, which will give you some insight into the role of Scripture in the process of spiritual formation. Then you should read the Overview, which will give you a sense of the main themes we discuss. The material in the chapters of this guide is intended to help you take the next step—to engage in activities that will help you grow closer to God.

INSTRUCTIONS FOR INDIVIDUALS

Because this book is an interactive guide for spiritual formation, we recommend that you read it more slowly than you would another kind of book. Read the Devotional and Scripture Readings and the My Life with God Exercise at the beginning of each chapter, then try to give yourself at least a week to do the exercise before reading the rest of the chapter. You may want to use a journal or notebook to record your responses to the questions in the chapter. Move on to a new chapter when you feel ready.

INSTRUCTIONS FOR GROUPS

If this is your first time participating in a spiritual formation group, your first question is likely: What *is* a spiritual formation group, anyway? Simply put, a spiritual formation group consists of two to seven people who meet together on a regular basis, bringing challenge and focus to their spiritual lives. Through mutual encouragement and accountability, spiritual formation groups enable their members to assist one another on the road of discipleship to Jesus Christ. We need encouragement during the times when we succeed and the times when we fail in our life of discipleship. We need others to keep us accountable, to remind us to continually pursue our lives with God and our discipleship to Jesus. Each is a natural by-product of the spiritual formation group experience.

If you are just starting a group, try recruiting one or two friends and asking each to recruit one other person. You could also place an ad in your church bulletin or make an announcement at your weekly service. Try to limit your group to seven people or fewer. With a larger group, meetings tend to run too long and not all members participate equally. Four or five people is optimal.

Plan for at least twelve group meetings, each dedicated to a chapter. (You might choose to have an additional introductory meeting or an extra final meeting for evaluation and making future plans.) Meet as often as once a week or as infrequently as once a month, whatever is best for your group. Each meeting should last sixty to ninety minutes. Although you may want to designate someone to be in charge of initial logistics and communication about meeting times and places, we have designed these guides to work in a leaderless format. Each week a different person serves as a facilitator to keep the discussion moving along. No extra study or preparation is required for that person; he or she simply follows the group directions in the margins of each chapter.

Before the first meeting, each member should read the Devotional and Scripture Readings and do the My Life with God Exercise in the first chapter. Because of these requirements and to make group meetings easier, it is helpful for each member of the group to have their own copy of this book. Members read ahead in this way before every meeting. The exercises are quite involved and require a time commitment of at least a few minutes each day over several days. Allow at least a week for members to do the exercise before holding the first meeting. Some may wish to read through the entire chapter beforehand, but it is not necessary to do so.

At the end of each chapter are additional exercises, resources, and reflection questions. These optional sections are primarily intended for individual use after the group meeting. Some may enjoy writing out answers to the reflection questions in the extra space provided or in their journals or notebooks. But if your group is quite interested in a particular chapter, you might consider incorporating the Additional Reflection Questions into your group meeting.

Now you are ready to form your group and plan your first meeting! May God bless you richly in this endeavor.

Lynda L. Graybeal and Julia L. Roller

THE WITH-GOD LIFE

Adapted from an essay in The Renovaré Spiritual Formation Bible *by Gayle Beebe, Richard J. Foster, Lynda L. Graybeal, Thomas C. Oden, and Dallas Willard*

CATCHING THE VISION: THE LIFE

The Bible is all about human life "with God." It is about how God has made this "with-God" life possible and will bring it to pass. In fact, the name Immanuel, meaning in Hebrew "God is with us," is the title given to the one and only Redeemer because it refers to God's everlasting intent for human life—namely, that we should be in every aspect a dwelling place of God. *Indeed, the unity of the Bible is discovered in the development of life with God as a reality on earth, centered in the person of Jesus.* We might call this the *Immanuel Principle* of life.

This dynamic, pulsating, with-God life is on nearly every page of the Bible. To the point of redundancy, we hear that *God is with* his people: with Abraham and Moses, with Esther and David, with Isaiah, Jeremiah, Amos, Micah, Haggai, and Malachi, with Mary, Peter, James, and John, with Paul and Barnabas, with Priscilla and Aquila, with Lydia, Timothy, Epaphroditus, Phoebe, and with a host of others too numerous to name.

Accordingly, the primary purpose of the RENOVARÉ guides is to enable us to see and understand the reality of the "with-God" life, to enter the process of the transformation of our whole person and of our whole life into *Christlikeness*.

Opening Ourselves to the Life

If we want to receive from the Bible the life "with God" that is portrayed *in* the Bible, we must be prepared to have our dearest and most fundamental assumptions about ourselves and our associations called into question. We must read humbly and in a constant attitude of repentance. Only in this way can we gain a thorough and practical grasp of the spiritual riches that God has made available to all humanity in his written Word.

When we turn to Scripture in this way, our reason for "knowing" the Bible and everything it teaches is that we might love more and know more of love.

We experience this love not as an abstraction but as a practical reality that possesses us. And because all those who love thoroughly obey the law, we would become ever more obedient to Jesus Christ and his Father.

Our goal is not to control the Bible—that is, to try to make it "come out right"—but simply to release its life into our lives and into our world. We seek to trust the living water that flows from Christ through the Bible, to open ourselves to this living water and to release it into the world as best we can, and then get out of its way.

NURTURING THE INTENTION: THE BIBLE

God remains with the Bible always. It is God's book. No one owns it but God himself. It is the loving heart of God made visible and plain. And receiving this message of exquisite love is the great privilege of all who long for life with God. *Reading, studying, memorizing, and meditating upon Scripture has always been the foundation of the Christian disciplines.* All of the disciplines are built upon Scripture. Our practice of the Spiritual Disciplines is kept on course by our immersion in Scripture. And so it is, we come to see, that this reading, studying, memorizing, and meditating is totally in the service of "the life which is life indeed" (1 Tim 6:19, RSV). We long with all our heart to know *for ourselves* this with-God kind of life that Jesus brings in all its fullness.

And the Bible has been given to help us. God has so superintended the writing of Scripture that it serves as a most reliable guide for our spiritual formation. But God uses human action in its presentation to the world, just as it is authored by humans. Thus we must consider how we ourselves can come to the Bible and also how we can present it to all peoples in a way that inducts the soul into the eternal kind of life.

We begin by finding experientially, day by day, how to let Jesus Christ live in every dimension of our being. In Christian community, we can open our lives to God's life by gathering regularly in little groups of two or more to encourage one another to discover the footprints of God in our daily existence and to venture out *with God* into areas where we have previously walked alone or not at all.

But the aim is not external conformity, whether to doctrine or deed, but the re-formation of the inner self—of the spiritual core, the place of thought and feeling, of will and character. The psalmist cries, "You desire truth in the inward being; therefore teach me wisdom in my secret heart. . . . Create in me a clean heart, O God, and put a new and right spirit within me" (Ps 51:6, 10). It is the "inner person" that is being "*renewed [renovaré] day by day*" (2 Cor 4:16, emphasis added).

While the many Christian traditions differ over the details of spiritual formation, they all come out at the same place: the transformation of the person into Christlikeness. "Spiritual formation" is the process of transforming the inner reality of the self (the *inward being* of the psalmist) in such a way that the overall life with God seen in the Bible naturally and freely comes to pass in us. Our inner world (the *secret heart*) becomes the home of Jesus, by his initiative and our response. As a result, our interior world becomes increasingly like the inner self of Jesus and, therefore, the natural source of words and deeds that are characteristic of him. By his enabling presence, we come to "let the same mind be in you that was in Christ Jesus" (Phil 2:5).

UNDERSTANDING THE MEANS: THE SPIRITUAL DISCIPLINES

This "with-God" life we find in the Bible is the very life to which we are called. In fact, it is exactly the life Jesus is referring to when he declares, "I am come that they might have life, and that they might have *it* more abundantly" (John 10:10, KJV). It is a life of unhurried peace and power. It is solid. It is serene. It is simple. It is radiant. It takes no time, though it permeates all of our time.

But such a life does not simply fall into our hands. Frankly, it is no more automatic for us than it was for those luminaries who walk across the pages of the Bible. There is a God-ordained way to become the kind of people and communities that can fully and joyfully enter into such abundant living. And this involves intentionally "train[ing] ... in godliness" (1 Tim 4:7). This is the purpose of the *disciplines* of the spiritual life. Indeed, the very reason for these spiritual formation guides is so that Scripture may be the primary means for the discovery, instruction, and practice of the Spiritual Disciplines, which bring us all the more fully into the with-God life.

The Spiritual Disciplines, then, are the God-ordained means by which each of us is enabled to bring the little, individualized power-pack we all possess—we call it the human body—and place it before God as "a living sacrifice" (Rom 12:1). It is the way we go about training in the spiritual life. By means of this process we become, through time and experience, the kind of person who naturally and freely expresses "love, joy, peace, patience, kindness, generosity, faithfulness, gentleness, and self-control" (Gal 5:22–23).

Many and Varied

What are these Spiritual Disciplines? They include fasting and prayer, study and service, submission and solitude, confession and worship, meditation and silence, simplicity, frugality, secrecy, sacrifice, and celebration. Such Spiritual Disciplines crop up repeatedly in the Bible as the way God's people trained themselves and were trained by God to achieve godliness. And not only in the Bible: the saints down through history, and even spilling over into our own time, have all practiced these ways of "grow[ing] in grace" (2 Pet 3:18).

A Spiritual Discipline is an intentionally directed action by which we do what we *can* do in order to receive from God the ability (or power) to do what we cannot achieve by direct effort. It is not in us, for example, to love our enemies. We might try very hard to love our enemies, but we will fail miserably. Always. This strength, this power to love our enemies—that is, to genuinely and unconditionally love those who curse us and spitefully use us—is simply not within our natural abilities. We cannot do it by ourselves. Ever.

But this *fact of life* does not mean that we do nothing. Far from it! Instead, by an act of the will we choose to take up disciplines of the spiritual life that we can do. These disciplines are all actions of body, mind, and spirit that are within our power. Not always and not perfectly, to be sure. But they are things we can do. By choice. By choosing actions of *fasting, study, solitude,* and so forth.

Their Purpose

The Spiritual Disciplines in and of themselves have no merit whatsoever. They possess no righteousness, contain no rectitude. Their purpose—their only purpose—is to place us before God. After that they have come to the end of their usefulness. But it is enough. Then the grace of God steps in and takes this simple offering of ourselves and creates out of it a person who embodies the goodness of God—indeed, a person who can come to the place of truly loving even enemies.

Again, Spiritual Disciplines involve doing what we *can* do to receive from God the power to do what we cannot do. And God graciously uses this process to produce in us the kind of person who automatically will do what needs to be done when it needs to be done.

Now, this ability to do what needs to be done when it needs to be done is the true freedom in life. Freedom comes not from the absence of restraint but from the presence of discipline. When we are on the spot, when we find ourselves in the midst of a crisis, it is too late. Training in the Spiritual Disciplines is the God-ordained means for forming and transforming the human personality so that when we are in a crisis we can be "response-able"—able to respond appropriately.

EXPERIENCING THE GRACE OF GOD:
THE EFFORT

It is vitally important for us to see all this spiritual training in the context of the work and action of God's grace. As the great apostle Paul reminds us, "It is God who is at work in you, enabling you both to will and to work for his good pleasure" (Phil 2:13). This, you see, is no "works righteousness," as it is sometimes called. Even our desire for this "with-God" kind of life is an action of grace; it is "prevenient grace," as the theologians say. You see, we are not just saved by grace, we live by grace. We pray by grace and fast by grace and study by grace and serve by grace and worship by grace. *All the disciplines are permeated by the enabling grace of God.*

But do not misunderstand—there *are* things for us to do. Daily. Grace never means inaction or total passivity. In ordinary life we will encounter many moments of decision when we must engage the will, saying "Yes!" to God's will and to God's way, as the People of God have done throughout history.

The opposite of grace is works, not effort. "Works" have to do with earning, and there simply is nothing any of us can do to earn God's love or acceptance. And, of course, we don't have to. God already loves us utterly and perfectly, and our complete acceptance is the free gift of God through Jesus Christ our Lord. In God's amazing grace, we live and move and have our being. But if we ever hope to "grow in grace," we will find ourselves engaging in effort of the most strenuous kind. As Jesus says, we are to "*strive* to enter through the narrow door" (Luke 13:24, emphasis added). And Peter urges us to "make every *effort* to support your faith with goodness, and goodness with knowledge, and knowledge with self-control, and self-control with endurance, and endurance with godliness, and godliness with mutual affection, and mutual affection with love" (2 Pet 1:5–7, emphasis added). It is this formation—indeed transformation—that we all desire.

TRAVELING WITH THE PEOPLE OF GOD:
THE JOURNEY

The luminaries who walk across the pages of our Bible not only practiced the various and sundry Spiritual Disciplines that formed—indeed transformed—them into Christlikeness, but did so while on a journey. The Bible records their lives as they traveled from the Garden of Eden to Canaan to Egypt to the Promised Land to Babylon and back. Then Jesus instructed the People of God to be his witnesses "to the ends of the earth" (Acts 1:8c), until they arrive at their final destination, "a new heaven and new earth" (Rev 21:1). During their travels God made himself known in various ways to the People of God wherever they were and whatever their social situation. They reacted to God's initiatives in many ways, sometimes rejoicing, at other times rebelling. This journey has been identified by the general editors of *The Renovaré Spiritual Formation Bible* as fifteen expressions of the with-God life (see the following chart). The book you hold in your hand illuminates one dimension, The People of God in Prayer and Worship. We hope it will help you understand how God has been with his people through the ages and continues to be with us today in our journey toward "the city that has foundations, whose architect and builder is God" (Heb 11:10).

THE PEOPLE OF GOD AND THE WITH-GOD LIFE*

Stage of Formation	Scriptures	God's Action	Human Reaction
I. The People of God in Individual Communion	Genesis 1–11**	Creates, instructs, steward of a good creation, banishes, destroys, restores	Disobey, rebel, sacrifice, murder, repent, obey
II. The People of God Become a Family	Genesis 12–50	Gives promise and establishes Abrahamic covenant, makes a great people	Faith, wrestle with God, persevere
III. The People of God in Exodus	Exodus, Leviticus, Numbers, Deuteronomy	Extends mercy, grace, and deliverance from exile; delivers the Mosaic covenant/law	Obey and disobey, develop a distinctive form of ritual
IV. The People of God in the Promised Land	Joshua, Judges, Ruth, 1 Samuel 1–12	Establishes a theocracy, bequeaths the Promised Land	Inhabit the Promised Land, accept judges as mediators
V. The People of God as a Nation	1 Samuel 13–31 & 2 Samuel, 1 & 2 Kings, 1 & 2 Chronicles, 1 Esdras 1	Permits the monarchy, exalts good kings, uses secular nations for blessing	Embrace the monarchy
VI. The People of God in Travail	Job, Psalms of Lament, Ecclesiastes, Lamentations, Tobit	Permits tribulation, allows suffering to strengthen faith	Complain yet remain faithful
VII. The People of God in Prayer and Worship	Psalms, Psalm 151	Establishes liturgical worship	Praise, prayer
VIII. The People of God in Daily Life	Proverbs, Ecclesiastes, Song of Solomon, Wisdom of Solomon, The Wisdom of Jesus Son of Sirach (Ecclesiasticus)	Gives precepts for living in community	Teachable, learning, treasure beautiful words and artistic expression
IX. The People of God in Rebellion	1 Kings 12–2 Kings 25:10, 2 Chronicles 10–36:19, Isaiah, Jeremiah 1–36, Hosea, Joel, Amos, Jonah, Micah, Nahum, Habakkuk, Zephaniah, Judith, Prayer of Manasseh	Proclaims prophetic judgment and redemption, reveals his rule over all nations, promises Immanuel, uses secular nations to bring judgment	Disbelieve and reject, believe false prophets, a faithful remnant emerges
X. The People of God in Exile	2 Kings 25:11–30, 2 Chronicles 36:20–23, Jeremiah 37–52, Lamentations, Ezekiel, Daniel, Obadiah, Baruch, Letter of Jeremiah, Additions to Daniel	Judges, yet remains faithful to covenant promises	Mourn, survive, long for Jerusalem, stand for God without institutions
XI. The People of God in Restoration	Ezra, Nehemiah, Esther, Daniel, Haggai, Zechariah, Malachi, Additions to Esther, 1 Esdras 2–9, & 2 Esdras, 1, 2, 3, & 4 Maccabees, Tobit, Additions to Daniel	Regathers and redeems, restructures social life	Return, obey, rebuild, worship, pursue Messianic figure, compile Septuagint
XII. The People of God with Immanuel	Matthew, Mark, Luke, John	Sends the Son and acts with the Son	Hear and follow, resist and reject
XIII. The People of God in Mission	Acts	Sends the Holy Spirit and creates the Church	Believe and proclaim, disbelieve and persecute
XIV. The People of God in Community	Romans, 1 & 2 Corinthians, Galatians, Ephesians, Philippians, Colossians, 1 & 2 Thessalonians, 1 & 2 Timothy, Titus, Philemon, Hebrews, James, 1 & 2 Peter, 1, 2, & 3 John, Jude	Builds, nurtures, and mobilizes the Church	Become disciples of Jesus Christ and make disciples to the ends of the earth
XV. The People of God into Eternity	Revelation	Reveals infinite progress toward infinite good	Worship and praise, creativity that magnifies God

* Text taken from *The Renovaré Spiritual Formation Bible.*

** Books are placed into categories by content, not by date of composition or type of literature.

Type of Mediation	Locus of Mediation	Social Context	Central Individual(s)	Key Spiritual Disciplines
Face-to-face	Garden, field, Noah's ark	Individuals	Adam, Eve, Enoch, Noah	Practicing the Presence, confession, sacrifice, obedience/submission
Through the family	Tent, desert, jail	Extended families and nomadic clans	Abraham and Sarah, Isaac, Jacob, Joseph	Pilgrimage, sacrifice, chastity
Through God's terrifying acts and the law	Ark of the covenant, tabernacle	Nomadic tribes	Moses	Submission, silence, simplicity, worship
Through the conquest and learning to act with God	Shiloh, Bethel	An ethnic people with fluid leadership	Joshua, Deborah, Ruth, Samson, Gideon, Samuel	Guidance, radical obedience/ submission, secrecy
Through the king, prophets, priests, and sacrifices	Altars, consecrated places, first (Solomonic) Temple	Political nation on the world stage	Saul, David, Hezekiah, Elijah, Elisha	Worship, prayer
Through suffering and the disappointments of life	Ash heap, hard circumstances of life	Individual	Job, Israel as the suffering servant	Fasting, solitude, silence, submission, service, celebration
Through song, prayer, worship	Jerusalem, flowering of individual experience	Nation	David	Prayer, worship, confession, celebration, meditation
Through wisdom	Temple, in the gate, home	Nation triumphant	Solomon	Study, guidance, celebration, meditation
Through the prophets and repression by the Gentiles	High places, Temple desecrated and destroyed	Nation under siege and dispersed	Isaiah, Hosea, Amos	Fasting, repentance, obedience/submission, solitude, silence, the law internalized
Through punishment, being a blessing to their captors	Babylon, anyplace, anytime	Ethnics abroad without a political homeland	Ezekiel, Jeremiah	Detachment, fasting, simplicity, prayer, silence, service
Through repentance, service, synagogue study	Rebuilt Temple, synagogue	Remnant on the international scene, ethnics in the leadership of other nations	Ezra, Cyrus the Persian, Nehemiah, Maccabees, Essenes, John the Baptist	Pilgrimage, confession, worship, study, service
Through the Incarnate Word and the living presence of the kingdom	Temple and synagogue, boats and hillsides, gatherings of disciples	Small groups, disciples, apostles, hostile critics	Jesus Christ Incarnate	Celebration, study, pilgrimage, submission, prayer, sacrifice, obedience, confession
Through the Holy Spirit, persecution, and martyrdom	Temple, synagogue, schools, riversides, public square	Jew, Gentile, house churches, abandonment of social strata	Peter, Paul	Speaking and hearing the word, sacrifice, guidance, generosity/ service, fasting, prayer
In one another, through Scripture, teaching, preaching, prophetic utterance, pastoral care, the Holy Spirit, the sacraments	Gathered community	Community redefined by the Body of Christ, decadent Greco-Roman culture	Peter, Paul, John	Prayer, study, accountability/ submission, fellowship
Throughout the cosmos	Focused in the New Jerusalem and extending throughout the cosmos	The Trinity and its community	God the Father, Son, and Holy Spirit; apostles, prophets	Living beyond disciplines

PRAYER AND WORSHIP: AN OVERVIEW

Prayer and worship are inextricably intertwined. When we come into the presence of God in prayer, something leads us to worship, and it seems worshiping God automatically moves us to pray. When we turn to the Bible, we see this pattern of prayer and worship ingrained in God's people. Hannah prays for a child while worshiping God (1 Sam 1:9–12). In his room Daniel worships and praises God three times a day (Dan 6:10b). Frequently Jesus goes away from the crowds to pray. And in Revelation John the apostle writes, "But the throne of God and the Lamb will be in it, and his servants will worship him" (22:3).

For this study we have chosen Scriptures that reflect the wedding of prayer and worship. Most of them come from Psalms, perhaps the most-loved book in the Bible, from which comes lines familiar to us in songs, prayers, and memorized verses. Psalms is a natural fit for a study of prayer and worship. For Christians, it is the prayerbook; for Jews, the songbook. Psalms encompasses the entire range of human emotions, from longing and repenting to lamenting and cursing to asking and thanking to praising and celebrating. We can never hope to cover all of the emotions and theology of prayer and worship here, but we have attempted to concentrate on the Scriptures we believe are most helpful for our spiritual formation in those areas. Rather than focusing on the type of Scripture or psalm, we explore what it says and how we can apply its teaching to our lives, always focusing on the practices of prayer and worship. Our goal is not to teach people how or why to pray or worship, but to open up new ways for us to enhance or renew our lives before God. Perhaps the greatest lesson the Scriptures teach us is that we should bring every part of our lives before God.

As we mentioned earlier, the psalms were used by the Israelites in worship, and they have continued to be an integral part of worship throughout the history of the Church and today. To honor these traditions, the Pointing to God section in each chapter focuses on someone who has influenced the worship life of the Church in some important way, whether as a musician, a composer, or a teacher.

May this guide help renew your life in the areas of prayer and worship!

1 LONGING

DEVOTIONAL READING

OS GUINNESS, *Long Journey Home*

"I'm at a point in my life where I realize there has to be something more."

The speaker, a man elegantly dressed, had come up to me after a dinner near San Francisco at which I'd been asked to give some remarks on the modern world's search for meaning. He cut straight to the point, and there was an intensity in his voice that immediately set him apart from the surrounding small talk.

"Like many of my friends around here," he continued, "I've learned a lesson I wish I'd known when I started out: Having it all just isn't enough. There's a limit to the successes worth counting and the toys worth accumulating. Business school never gave me a calculus for assessing the deeper things of life."

Many of the guests at the dinner were eminent names from the world of high finance in the city and the world of high technology in Silicon Valley further south. Their conversation was flush with the success of the twentieth century's last two decades, a period that witnessed the greatest legal creation of wealth in history, much of it in that very corner of the world.

In my remarks to them, I hadn't uttered the phrase "something more." But in separate conversations with me afterward, no fewer than four people—each with a very different story—used those very words to express their sense of longing. As it happens so often in life, the very things they had striven to achieve turned out to be, once achieved, far less than enough.

I've had similar conversations in living rooms, classrooms, cafés, pubs, airplanes, and trains across the world. As G. K. Chesterton wrote: "We all feel the riddle of the earth without anyone to point it out. The

It is helpful for everyone to read the Devotional and Scripture Readings and do the My Life with God Exercise before the meeting. Begin the meeting with silent prayer, then move directly to Reflecting on My Life with God below.

mystery of life is the plainest part of it." Nothing is more human for people of all backgrounds—for all of us—than a desire to unriddle our life's mystery. . . .

The very fact that we desire is proof that we are creatures. We're incomplete in ourselves, so we desire whatever we think is beckoning to complete us.

We're therefore right to desire happiness but wrong to think that happiness may be found wherever our desires lead us. Only the true God can satisfy desire, for God alone needs nothing outside himself; he himself is the highest and the only lasting good. So all objects we desire, short of God, are either false (because they're unreal) or as finite and incomplete as we ourselves are—and therefore disappointing, if we make them the objects of ultimate desire.

True satisfaction and real rest can be found only in the highest and most lasting good, so all seeking short of the pursuit of God brings only restlessness. As St. Augustine confessed to him, "You have made us only for yourself, and our hearts are restless until they find their rest in you."[1]

MY LIFE WITH GOD EXERCISE

If we are honest with ourselves, we will admit that even those of us who have committed to a relationship with God long for many other things: to marry the perfect person, to have security, to have job success, to keep our families safe, to be happy. These longings are not wrong in and of themselves, yet, as the people Guinness met acknowledged and our own experiences tell us, focusing all our energies on achieving these goals still leaves us unsatisfied, lonely, and longing for something more. Think about some times in the past when you achieved or acquired something you thought you wanted more than anything. How did you feel afterward? Was it as satisfying as you had anticipated? Take a moment now to search your heart. What are the objects you are seeking and longing for at this time in your life? Are they the things you truly want? Carefully consider. Is it possible that you are misdirecting your longing to know more and experience more of God into something else?

Guinness tells us that only God can satisfy desire. Making success or security or prosperity or even happiness our ultimate goal can lead only to restlessness. But he also assures us that God reaches down to us even as we confusedly reach out to other things. As John of the Cross wrote, "The longing in your soul is actually His doing. You may feel only the smallest desire for Him. There may be no emotion about it at all. But the reason your desire rises at all is because He is passing very near to you. His holy beauty comes near you, like a spiritual scent, and it stirs your drowsing soul."[2]

Each day this week seek to pay attention to God's stirrings of your drowsing soul by reading or singing the worship song "As the Deer" by Martin Nystrom:

As the deer panteth for the water
So my soul longeth after Thee.
You alone are my heart's desire,
And I long to worship Thee.
[Refrain]

You alone are my strength, my shield,
To You alone may my spirit yield.
You alone are my heart's desire,
And I long to worship Thee.

You're my friend and You are my brother
Even though You are a king.
I love You more than any other,
So much more than anything.
[Refrain]

I want You more than gold or silver,
Only You can satisfy.
You alone are the real joy giver
And the apple of my eye.[3]
[Refrain]

Throughout the week, think about the different times in your life when you have felt especially thirsty for God. Looking back, can you see what in your life caused those feelings? Were you longing for God because your soul felt particularly barren or empty, or did your longings come from a place of being especially close to God? How did you try to feed your soul's longings?

What insight about yourself did you gain while doing the exercise? How would you describe the current state of your heart? Dry? Longing?

REFLECTING ON MY LIFE WITH GOD
Allow each member a few moments to answer this question.

➤ SCRIPTURE READING: PSALM 42:1–8

After everyone has had a chance to respond to the question, ask a member to read this passage from Scripture.

As a deer longs for flowing streams,
    so my soul longs for you, O God.
My soul thirsts for God,
    for the living God.
When shall I come and behold
    the face of God?
My tears have been my food
    day and night,
while people say to me continually,
    "Where is your God?"

These things I remember
    as I pour out my soul:
how I went with the throng,
    and led them in procession to the house of God,
with glad shouts and songs of thanksgiving,
    a multitude keeping festival.
Why are you cast down, O my soul,
    and why are you disquieted within me?
Hope in God; for I shall again praise him,
    my help and my God.

My soul is cast down within me;
    therefore I remember you
from the land of Jordan and of Hermon,
    from Mount Mizar.
Deep calls to deep
    at the thunder of your cataracts;
all your waves and your billows
    have gone over me.
By day the LORD commands his steadfast love,
    and at night his song is with me,
    a prayer to the God of my life.

REFLECTION QUESTION
Allow each person a few moments to respond to this question.

What emotions does this psalm evoke in you? How does the water image the psalmist uses fit with your own experience of longing for God?

▶▶ GETTING THE PICTURE

✍ After a brief discussion, choose one person to read this section.

Psalm 42 is an individual's prayerful lament as he longs to return to Jerusalem, where he can serve and worship God in his vocation as a musician in the Temple. Most likely he was taken to Babylon in 582 BC as a captive with other leaders and royalty. The tone of the psalm and the questions he asks suggest a permanent separation from his homeland. He describes continually facing the sneering taunts of the Babylonians, who ask, "Where is your God?" In response, the psalmist asks God why he has been abandoned and wonders why his soul is so discouraged and unsettled. In spite of the doubts that the taunts plant in his heart, he comes back to the refrain, "Hope in God; for I shall again praise him, my help and my God."

Historically, Psalm 42 was most likely combined with Psalm 43. Both psalms have been attributed to the Korahites, who served as singers, gatekeepers, and bakers at the Solomonic Temple. Major themes in both psalms include the repeated phrase "Where is your God?"; recollections of places the psalmist remembers—for example, Mount Mizar and the "altar of God"; and a deep interest in worship, which centers on joyfully leading a procession to God's house (42:4) and praising God by playing his harp before the altar (43:4).

Likely the first verse is the most familiar. Here the psalmist sets the tenor for the rest of the poem: "As a deer longs for flowing streams, so my soul longs for you, O God." The psalmist takes for granted that the worshipers know the habits of deer. During the daytime deer hide in brush and trees, where there is no water. Toward evening they leave their hiding places to graze in the valleys, where grass and water are plentiful. When they arrive at the stream, predators could be lurking about, and they might have to wait in the brush until the danger subsides. In either case, the deer would be very thirsty before they could satisfy their thirst with the cool water of a rushing stream. It is this thirst that the palmist equates with his own soul's thirst for the living God.

▶▶▶ GOING DEEPER

✍ Have another member read this section.

It becomes clear from reading Psalm 42 that our life comes from God and is meant to be lived with God. While using the metaphor of water in different forms—streams, cataracts, waves, billows—the psalmist recognized that water was not the source of his life; rather, God was. And God is alive (v 2). This was in direct contrast to the beliefs of the Babylonians, among whom the psalmist was living in exile. They worshiped idols made of gold and silver and wood and stone, idols that could not see or hear or respond. In contrast, the *living* God was able to interact with the psalmist and give him what he needed, namely, *living* water. Jesus promises us the same: "The water that I will give will become in them a spring of water gushing up to eternal life" (John 4:14).

The psalm also reveals that worship of God is an essential part of our with-God life and a natural outpouring of our longing for God. This worship is joyful; it is filled with "glad shouts and songs of thanksgiving" in the midst of the gathering of believers. It lifts our spirits and leads us to thank God for all the goodness and grace we find in our lives. May we, along with the psalmist, shout our praises to God!

We also learn from this psalm that regardless of whether we feel his presence, God is with us in bad times and good, day and night. Just as it is natural for a deer to long for water when thirsty, so it is natural for us to ask questions and pour out our souls to God when we feel abandoned or distant from him. The psalmist was almost a thousand miles from the Temple in Jerusalem where he had helped lead worship. He remembered worshiping God and feeling the joy that filled his heart during those services. Nothing in the land of his captivity could compare to it. There were no festivals in Babylon to gather the Israelites three times a year to worship God. There was no Temple. Even his beloved Temple back in Jerusalem had been destroyed. But after remembering the times of worship, he asked himself why he despaired (v 5). Though everything in the short term looked bleak, he knew that he would once again praise God. In all circumstances of life, no matter what the world throws at us, we can live in hope because we know that God will go through anything we face with us. God is "a very present help in trouble" (Ps 46:1).

REFLECTION QUESTION
Allow each person a few moments to respond.

Have you had an experience where you felt separated from God by your circumstances? What does the psalm say to the condition of your soul then and now?

▶▶▶ POINTING TO GOD

✐ Choose one member to read this section.

From Gregory the Great to Handel to Charles Wesley, generation upon generation of Christians have put different musical stamps on praise and worship, often by taking words or verses from the psalms and building upon them with varying lyrics, keys, harmonies, and background accompaniments. The song we focused on in this chapter's exercise, "As the Deer," is an example of today's contemporary worship movement, which features songs written in the first person ("I") and melodies sung in unison or with a simple two-part harmony, often accompanied by instruments such as guitars, keyboards, and drums. John Wimber was one of the pioneers of the contemporary worship movement.

Wimber, the founder of the Vineyard community of churches, had been a rock musician and a member of the Righteous Brothers. But in the 1970s, he had a conversion experience when he was participating in a Quaker Bible study, and he gave up his rock career. He and his wife, Carol, began a small home church, which would eventually become the Anaheim Vineyard. In this intimate setting they started to rethink their ideas about worship. "I noticed times during the meeting—usually when we sang—in which I experienced God deeply," said Carol. "We sang many songs, but mostly songs about worship or testimonies from one Christian to another. But occasionally we sang a song personally and intimately to Jesus, with lyrics like 'Jesus I love you.' Those types of songs both stirred and fed the hunger for God within me. About this time I began asking our music leader why some songs seemed to spark something in us and others didn't. As we talked about worship, we realized that often we would sing about worship yet we never actually worshipped—except when we accidentally stumbled onto intimate songs like 'I Love You Lord,' and 'I Lift My Voice.' Thus we began to see a difference between songs about Jesus and songs to Jesus."[4] They also realized that worship of God involved their bodies as well, through actions such as singing, playing instruments, dancing, kneeling, and lifting hands.

With these insights about worship at its core, Vineyard Music was born. John started to write worship songs, including "Isn't He?", "To Seek Your Face," and "Worthy Is the Lamb." Many other musicians also recorded their songs with Vineyard Music Group. One of the common threads running through these songs is a longing, a hunger, to experience God. Many of the lyrics speak of wanting to see God, to touch Jesus, to feel God in a new way. Through John's preaching and speaking, and always through the music, Vineyard Churches spread throughout the world. All the while, John emphasized simplicity in worship and keeping the focus on Jesus. He believed that as long as worship came from an outpouring of the spirit, it would always be relevant, and that it was okay for worship styles to change from generation to generation.

As a result of the work of John Wimber and other influential musicians and groups, such as Don Moen, Paul Baloche, Integrity Music Group, and Maranatha!, today the contemporary praise service is the standard in many churches.

▶▶▶▶▶ GOING FORWARD

🕊 Have another person read this section.

Longing is a common thread woven through our prayer and worship, from the psalms to contemporary praise music today. We long to be closer to God, to experience ever more of him, for his presence to remain strongly with us in times of trouble as well as times of prosperity. This longing for God is not simply a stage in our faith journey; it is a constant in the with-God life. As A. W. Tozer writes,

> To have found God and still to pursue Him is the soul's paradox of love, scorned indeed by the too-easily-satisfied religionist, but justified in happy experience by the children of the burning heart.... Come near to the holy men and women of the past and you will soon feel the heat of their desire after God. They mourned for Him, they prayed and wrestled and sought for Him day and night, in season and out, and when they had found Him the finding was all the sweeter for the long seeking.... I want deliberately to encourage this mighty longing after God. The lack of it has brought us to our present low estate. The stiff and wooden quality about our religious lives is a result of our lack of holy desire. Complacency is a deadly foe of all spiritual growth. Acute desire must be present or there will be no manifestation of Christ to His people. He waits to be wanted. Too bad that with many of us He waits so long, so very long, in vain.[5]

Unlike those called "seekers" in modern parlance, who don't really know what they are looking for, we are seekers with a purpose—seeking to know more and more about the God we love. For where are we when we stop desiring to grow closer to God, to know more of him? Embrace your yearnings, your longings for God. Express them to him. Ask to be more and more filled with his loving Spirit, for your cup to run over. Picture yourself as dry, parched land, eager to soak up God's living water. Sing these yearnings to the Lord. As the apostle Paul advises us: "Be filled with the Spirit, as you sing psalms and hymns and spiritual songs among yourselves, singing and making melody to the Lord in your hearts, giving thanks to God the Father at all times and for everything in the name of our Lord Jesus Christ" (Eph 5:18b–20).

Describe a worship experience during which you were in touch with your longing for God. What kind of music was being used? Were there life circumstances influencing your mood? What, if any, was the lasting effect?

This concludes our look at longing. In the next chapter we will turn our attention to another avenue of prayer and worship—exhorting.

REFLECTION QUESTION
Again, allow each member a few moments to answer this question.

✍ After everyone has had a chance to respond, the leader reads this paragraph.

CLOSING PRAYER

Incline your ear, O Lord, and answer me,
    for I am poor and needy,
Preserve my life, for I am devoted to you;
    save your servant who trusts in you.
You are my God; be gracious to me, O Lord,
    for to you do I cry all day long.
Gladden the soul of your servant,
    for to you, O Lord, I lift up my soul.
For you, O Lord, are good and forgiving,
    abounding in steadfast love to all who call on you.
Give ear, O Lord, to my prayer;
    listen to my cry of supplication.
In the day of my trouble I call on you,
    for you will answer me.

For you are great and do wondrous things;
    you alone are God.
Teach me your way, O Lord,
    that I may walk in your truth. (PS 86:1–7, 10–11a)

✍ **Allow some time for members to encourage one another to read the Devotional and Scripture Readings and do the exercise in the following chapter before the next meeting.** Then invite the members to be silent for a few moments before leading them in reading the Closing Prayer aloud together.

✍ At the end of the Closing Prayer, the leader asks for a volunteer to lead the next meeting.

TAKING IT FURTHER

Write your own psalm (you can think of it as a poem if that is helpful) about longing for God. What images come to you? Images of water or other images?

ADDITIONAL EXERCISE

ADDITIONAL RESOURCES

Carney, Glandion, and William Long. *Longing for God: Prayer and the Rhythms of Life*. Downers Grove, IL: InterVarsity, 1993.

Macy, Howard R. *Rhythms of the Inner Life*. Colorado Springs, CO: Cook Communications/Chariot Victor, 1999.

Peterson, Eugene H. *Answering God*. San Francisco: HarperSanFrancisco, 1989.

ADDITIONAL REFLECTION QUESTIONS

What forms has longing for God taken in your life? Do you periodically find your soul growing dry and barren because your schedule is too busy? If so, what might you do to help yourself stop that cycle?

In terms of your longing for God, would you call yourself a seeker or a finder or a combination of both?

Does singing to God in the second person ("you"), as we find in so many contemporary praise songs, or singing to God in the third person ("him" or "he" or "God"), as is often the case in hymns, make a difference to you? What different feelings and sense of worship are evoked by each?

EXHORTING

2

DEVOTIONAL READING

MARTIN LUTHER, "A Simple Way to Pray"

Dear Master Peter:

I will tell you as best I can what I do personally when I pray. May our dear Lord grant to you and to everybody to do it better than I! Amen.

First, when I feel that I have become cool and joyless in prayer because of other tasks or thoughts (for the flesh and the devil always impede and obstruct prayer), I take my little Psalter, hurry to my room, or, if it be the day and hour for it, to the church where a congregation is assembled and, as time permits, I say quietly to myself and word-for-word the Lord's Prayer, Ten Commandments, the Creed, and, if I have time, some words of Christ or of Paul, or some psalms, just as a child might do.

It is a good thing to let prayer be the first business of the morning and the last at night. Guard yourself carefully against those false, deluding ideas that tell you, *Wait a little while. I will pray in an hour; first I must attend to this or that.* Such thoughts get you away from prayer into other affairs, which so hold your attention and involve you that nothing comes of prayer for that day.

It may well be that you may have some tasks which are as good or better than prayer, especially in an emergency. There is a saying ascribed to St. Jerome that everything a believer does is prayer, and a proverb says, "Those who work faithfully pray twice." This can be said because believers fear and honor God in their work and remember the commandment not to wrong anyone, or to try to steal, defraud, or cheat. Such thoughts and such faith undoubtedly transform their work into prayer and a sacrifice of praise.

Christ commands continual prayer:

> Ask, and it will be given to you; seek and you will find; knock, and it will be opened to you. For everyone who asks receives, and

🕊 It is helpful for everyone to read the Devotional and Scripture Readings and do the My Life with God Exercise before the meeting. Begin the meeting with silent prayer, then move directly to Reflecting on My Life With God below.

he who seeks finds, and to him who knocks it will be opened. If his son asks for bread, will [he] give him a stone? Or if he asks for a fish, will he give him a serpent? If you then, being evil, know how to give good gifts to your children, how much more will your Father give the Holy Spirit to those who ask Him! (Luke 11:9–13)

.... One must unceasingly guard against sin and wrongdoing, something one cannot do unless one fears God and keeps His commandments in mind, as the psalmist says, *"Blessed are those ... who meditate on his law day and night"* (Psalm 1:1–2). Yet we must be careful not to break the habit of true prayer and imagine other works to be necessary which, after all, are nothing of the kind. Thus at the end we become lax and lazy, cool and listless toward prayer. The devil who besets us is not lazy or careless, and our flesh is too ready and eager to sin and is disinclined to the spirit of prayer.

When your heart has been warmed by such recitation to yourself (of the Ten Commandments, the words of Christ, etc.) and is intent upon the matter, kneel or stand with your hands folded and your eyes toward heaven and speak or think as briefly as you can.

Prayer According to God's Commands and Promises

O heavenly Father, dear God, I am a poor unworthy sinner. I do not deserve to raise my eyes or hands toward You or to pray. But because You have commanded us all to pray and have promised to hear us and through Your dear Son, Jesus Christ, have taught us both how and what to pray, I come to you in obedience to Your Word, trusting in your gracious promises.

I pray in the name of my Lord Jesus Christ together with all Your saints and Christians on earth as He has taught us:

> Our Father in heaven, hallowed be your Name. Your kingdom come. Your will be done on earth as it is in heaven. Give us this day our daily bread. And forgive us our debts, as we forgive our debtors. And do not lead us into temptation, but deliver us from the evil one. For Yours is the kingdom and the power and the glory forever. Amen (Matthew 6:5-13).[1]

MY LIFE WITH GOD EXERCISE

In this letter written in 1535, Martin Luther gives advice to Peter Beskendorf, his barber, about when, how, why, and what to pray. At this time Luther had been a teacher at the University of Wittenberg and the pastor of Wittenberg Church for more than twenty years and had known the master barber for at least eighteen years. Luther's health had been deteriorating since 1527, probably exacerbated by the stress of a busy schedule and constant opposition to his teachings by the Catholic Church. In addition to his jobs as a teacher—and later dean of the theological faculty—and pastor, Luther went on preaching tours; wrote books, tracts, sermons, and song lyrics; translated the Bible and liturgy into German; published books; read voraciously; and participated in an active family life. Yet, he was still able to find time to write personal letters containing spiritual advice to friends of long standing.

Because the advice in the letter to Master Peter is so unusual, we ask you to experiment with Luther's method of prayer. Begin with a recitation of at least some of the Scriptures he mentions, and perhaps the Apostles' Creed. Next "kneel or stand with your hands folded and your eyes toward heaven" and recite Luther's prayer, finishing, as he does, with the Lord's Prayer. You may not be able to recite everything Luther suggests each time you pray, but try his method at least two or three times. To prepare for your prayer time, you will need to put bookmarks in your Bible at the Ten Commandments (Exod 20:1–17) and your favorite passage(s) from the Psalms, Gospels, or Epistles. Here is the Apostles' Creed:

> I believe in God,
> > The Father Almighty,
> > Maker of heaven and earth;
> And in Jesus Christ
> > His only Son our Lord;
> > Who was conceived by the Holy Spirit,
> > Born of the Virgin Mary,
> > Suffered under Pontius Pilate,
> > Was crucified, died, and was buried;
> > He descended into hell;
> > The third day He rose again from the dead;
> > He ascended into heaven,
> > And sits on the right hand of God the Father Almighty;
> > From where He shall come to judge the living and the dead.
> I believe in
> > The Holy Spirit;
> > The holy catholic* Church;

* i.e., universal.

The communion of saints;
The forgiveness of sins;
The resurrection of the body;
And the life everlasting. Amen.

REFLECTING ON MY LIFE WITH GOD
Allow each member a few moments to answer this question.

What was your experience with Luther's prayer method?

▶ SCRIPTURE READING: PSALM 37:1–9, 25–28

After everyone has had a chance to respond to the question, ask a member to read this passage from Scripture.

Do not fret because of the wicked;
    do not be envious of wrongdoers,
for they will soon fade like the grass,
    and wither like the green herb.

Trust in the LORD, and do good;
    so you will live in the land, and enjoy security.
Take delight in the LORD,
    and he will give you the desires of your heart.

Commit your way to the LORD;
    trust in him, and he will act.
He will make your vindication shine like the light,
    and the justice of your cause like the noonday.

Be still before the LORD, and wait patiently for him;
    do not fret over those who prosper in their way,
    over those who carry out evil devices.

Refrain from anger, and forsake wrath.
    Do not fret—it leads only to evil.
For the wicked shall be cut off,
    but those who wait for the LORD shall inherit the land....

I have been young, and now am old,
    yet I have not seen the righteous forsaken
    or their children begging bread.
They are ever giving liberally and lending,
    and their children become a blessing.

Depart from evil, and do good;
      so you shall abide forever.
For the LORD loves justice;
      he will not forsake his faithful ones.

What stands out most to you in this exhortation, or teaching?

REFLECTION QUESTION
Allow each person a few moments to respond to this question.

➤➤ GETTING THE PICTURE

Leaders from the birth of the Church onward have often taught by exhorting, which means strongly encouraging or urging someone to do something. Exhorting comes in many forms, both sacred and secular: a letter from a good friend, like the one Martin Luther sent to his barber; a sermon; an advertisement or infomercial on television or radio; the lyrics of a song; a book; a movie trailer on the Internet; or a scriptural passage. The above biblical exhortation is a wisdom psalm. As is typical of wisdom literature in the Bible, such as Proverbs, in this psalm a teacher is trying to pass on what he knows about the with-God life to us, his students. The psalmist tells us that he is old, which means that he is to be accorded the authority and respect due to people of age in the Israelite culture, and that his exhortation comes from what he has seen and experienced in his long life. The sharp contrast he draws between the wicked and the righteous is also typical of wisdom literature.

✍ After a brief discussion, choose one person to read this section.

    The psalmist offers many specific pieces of advice, but his overall message is that those who follow the Lord, who delight in him, will be rewarded by God. This psalm is addressed to the people of Israel, who had inherited the land of Canaan but were faced every day with people in their midst who were "wicked." Although, as we read in so many psalms, the wicked may prosper temporarily, God does not forsake those who follow his ways. The second and third stanzas are the centerpiece of the psalm:

    Trust in the LORD, and do good;
        so you will live in the land, and enjoy security.
    Take delight in the LORD,
        and he will give you the desires of your heart.

    Commit your way to the LORD;
        trust in him, and he will act.

Trust in the Lord, take delight in him, and commit your way to him—three important exhortations. We see that the exhortation to trust in the Lord is immediately preceded by an assurance that evildoers and the wicked will wither like grass; in this context trusting means knowing that the Lord is in charge. It is not our job to even be concerned about those around us who are doing evil; we are called instead to focus on our own kingdom work, to "do good" and to trust that God will take care of the rest. In the Israelite economy, doing good meant being honest in your business dealings (Prov 3:27), showing common sense (Prov 12:8), giving worthwhile advice (Prov 12:26), having virtuous plans (Prov 14:22), and the like.

We are next urged to take delight in the Lord, which will lead to the desires of our heart being fulfilled. As we discussed in the first chapter, God is the only one who can satisfy our innermost desires and longings. So much of our unhappiness stems from expecting other things to fulfill us. We can assume that in the course of the psalmist's long life he learned from experience that seeking after things other than God leads only to restlessness, never to fulfillment. The phrase he uses, to "take delight in the LORD," evokes the joy and fulfillment we find in God.

Next, the psalmist urges us to commit our way to God. This ongoing commitment is to be taken very seriously. The following lines make clear that we can expect challenges. We will see things that anger us, times when evil seems victorious. But we must remain firm in our commitment, and that takes patience, not flying off the handle or giving up on God when things temporarily look bleak. This commitment is a long-term one, and it requires trusting that things will work out according to God's plan. Even over one lifetime, the psalmist has seen that the righteous are rewarded for their patience and commitment.

▶▶▶ GOING DEEPER

Have another member read this section.

Exhortations such as this psalm demonstrate that exhortation is a duty of leaders and a privilege for all believers to receive. Through the many vehicles of exhortation, we receive wisdom that has been refined by countless hours of sitting and waiting before God. The words of the psalmists in 67, 81, 95, and 146–50; Solomon and Lemuel in Proverbs; the prophets; Paul; Jesus; and those of his inner circle, Peter, James, and John, continue to ring with truth and encouragement. Books by the spiritual masters Thomas à Kempis, Madame Guyon, Thomas Kelley, Julian of Norwich, Jean-Pierre de Caussade, Evelyn Underhill, and Dietrich Bonhoeffer guide us in our walk with Christ. Sermons by the reformers John Wesley, John Calvin, and Martin Luther; contemporary teachers; and our own pastors feed our souls and help us attain our goal of becoming like Christ as we journey through life.

With all the teachings vying for our attention, how can we determine which exhortations to follow? First, we must take a close look at the source of the exhortation, even while recognizing that truth often comes to us from unexpected places. The psalmist noted his old age as evidence of his wisdom, and we should certainly respect those with a great deal of life experience. We also know, however, that advanced age does not always herald wisdom, nor does youth necessarily indicate the lack of it. The fruits of one's life with God are a better indicator of wisdom. As Dallas Willard writes, "All one has to do to identify those who would mislead us is watch what they do and pay little attention to what they say. What they do will be the unerring sign of who they are on the inside."[2] Further, wise persons are those who admit that they do not know everything, who are humble before God. According to Psalm 111:10, "The fear of the LORD is the beginning of wisdom; / all those who practice it have a good understanding."

Most importantly, we must examine the message, holding up all writings and verbal exhortations to the searching light of the biblical witness and praying for God's constant guidance. We must be reluctant to accept quick fixes or easy steps to better prayer or more success. Conversely, there are times when we will be all too eager to deny or reject an exhortation. It is hard sometimes to accept the counsel of another, especially when their advice sets us on a difficult path. As the psalmist made clear, our path requires patience and trust.

At times we will also be in the position of offering an exhortation, particularly those of us who are leaders or teachers. We can learn from the tone struck by the psalmist. His words were gentle and filled with hope and reassurance, yet he did not promise ease or present-day happiness, only that God would reward the righteous in his own time. We, like Jesus, should "not break a bruised reed or quench a smoldering wick" when urging people to become more like him (Matt 12:20).

What teacher has been most influential in your life of discipleship to Jesus?

REFLECTION QUESTION
Allow each person a few moments to respond.

▶▶▶▶ POINTING TO GOD

An important figure who has taught generations of Christians about worship is British writer Evelyn Underhill. In 1911, in her book *Mysticism*,

↶ Choose one member to read this section.

she described mysticism as a gradual awakening of the self to God. Her ability to make this esoteric topic accessible to a wide audience made Underhill a sought-after lecturer and writer. But despite her professional success, Underhill began to feel that something was missing in her spiritual life. She had focused her gaze inward, to the exclusion of outward disciplines, such as service and participation in the life of a church community.

She rejoined the Church of England, which she had attended as a child, and sought out Baron Friedrich von Hugel, a Roman Catholic spiritual director. Von Hugel agreed with Underhill's self-assessment and recommended that she add to her spiritual practice outward disciplines such as visiting the poor on a regular basis and cultivating a nonreligious hobby. His direction helped Underhill to experience her faith from her heart as well as her head; she later credited von Hugel with reigniting her love for Christ. Gradually, Underhill's spiritual life gained balance. She liked to quote St. Teresa's saying that "to give Our Lord a perfect service Martha and Mary must combine." In her life this took the form of devoting her mornings to writing and her afternoons to teaching and service work. Her return to the Church and to corporate worship was a turning point for Underhill, leading her to write *Worship,* her best-known and most influential work. Whereas *Mysticism,* written at the beginning of Underhill's career, dealt primarily with the interior life of the individual, *Worship* was the fruit of her years of service and teaching in community.

Like von Hugel, Underhill began to see her calling as aiding others in their spiritual lives. To this end, she led retreats and served as a spiritual director, while continuing to write thirty books. As a teacher, she had a horror of "pushing souls about," but at the same time she was firmly committed to helping people grow at God's pace rather than their own or her own, a sentiment that endeared her to her students. Her skill in spiritual direction and the heart of her teaching about worship comes through in this portion of a letter she wrote to one of her directees in 1937:

> I feel the regular, steady, docile practice of corporate worship is of the utmost importance for the building-up of your spiritual life: more important, really, than the reading of advanced books like De Caussade [*Abandonment to Divine Providence*], though I am delighted that he attracts and helps you and feeds your soul. But no amount of solitary reading makes up for humble immersion in the life and worship of the Church. In fact the books are only addressed to those who are taking part in that life. The corporate and personal together make up the Christian ideal. You will find the "new atti-

tude" you speak of—the simplicity, trust, and dependence—can be kept up, and that your Communions will play a very important part here, giving support of a kind you can hardly get in any other way, reminding you too of the great life of the Church, engulfing your little life, and checking any tendency to individualism.[3]

▶▶▶▶▶ GOING FORWARD

An essential part of our life as Christians is the teachings and exhortations we receive from the Bible, great spiritual writers throughout the ages, and the words of our pastors and friends. Though, as Underhill writes, solitary reading is not meant to take the place of participation in corporate worship, learning from the great spiritual masters is an important part of our faith journey. Further, most of us attend worship services that center around a Scripture reading and an exhortation based on that Scripture. We may also participate in small groups where we study the Scriptures and learn from each other's insights, revealing that we have much to learn and much to teach each other, and we can encourage one another as we pursue the life of faith.

What is the role of exhorting in your church?

This concludes our look at exhorting. In the next chapter we will turn our attention to another avenue of prayer and worship—repenting.

> ✍ Have another person read this section.

> **REFLECTION QUESTION**
> Again, allow each member a few moments to answer this question.

> ✍ After everyone has had a chance to respond, the leader reads this paragraph.

> ✍ Allow some time for members to encourage one another to read the Devotional and Scripture Readings and do the exercise in the following chapter before the next meeting. Then invite the members to be silent for a few moments before leading them in reading the Closing Prayer aloud together.

CLOSING PRAYER

Incline your ear, O LORD, and answer me,
    for I am poor and needy,
Preserve my life, for I am devoted to you;
    save your servant who trusts in you.
You are my God; be gracious to me, O Lord,
    for to you do I cry all day long.
Gladden the soul of your servant,
    for to you, O Lord, I lift up my soul.
For you, O Lord, are good and forgiving,
    abounding in steadfast love to all who call on you.

◁ At the end of the Closing Prayer, the leader asks for a volunteer to lead the next meeting.

Give ear, O LORD, to my prayer;
>   listen to my cry of supplication.
In the day of my trouble I call on you,
>   for you will answer me.

For you are great and do wondrous things;
>   you alone are God.
Teach me your way, O LORD,
>   that I may walk in your truth. (PS 86:1–7, 10–11a)

TAKING IT FURTHER

ADDITIONAL EXERCISE

Meditate on Psalm 37 in its entirety for at least a week. Read it each day, perhaps focusing on a different stanza each time. Write down any thoughts and insights in your journal.

ADDITIONAL RESOURCES

Luther, Martin. *Luther's Works*. Vol. 43, edited by Gustav Wiencke. Minneapolis, MN: Augsburg Fortress, 1968.

Parrish, Archie. *A Simple Way to Pray*. Marietta, GA: Serve International, 2005.

Underhill, Evelyn. *Essential Writings*. Edited by Emilie Griffin. Maryknoll, NY: Orbis, 2003.

Underhill, Evelyn. *Worship*. Eugene, OR: Wipf and Stock, 1989.

Webber, Robert E. *Worship Is a Verb*. Waco, TX: Word, 1985.

ADDITIONAL REFLECTION QUESTIONS

How have you practiced the gift of exhortation? Through your conversation and counsel? Through your intuitive grasp of difficult theological teachings? Through actions such as teaching a Sunday school class or leading a small group?

In what ways have you learned the most about God? Communally as a member of your congregation? In fellowship as a member of a small group? Individually while reading Christian books or studying Scripture? As a student in school or seminary? What insight does this give you about your beliefs?

What are some of the negative exhortations that have influenced and continue to influence you?

REPENTING

3

DEVOTIONAL READING

EUGENE H. PETERSON, *A Long Obedience in the Same Direction*

The first step toward God is a step away from the lies of the world. It is a renunciation of the lies we have been told about ourselves and our neighbors and our universe....

The usual biblical word describing the no we say to the world's lies and the yes we say to God's truth is *repentance*. It is always and everywhere the first word in the Christian life. John the Baptist's preaching was, "Repent, for the kingdom of heaven is at hand" (Mt 3:2, RSV). Jesus' first preaching was the same: "Repent, for the kingdom of heaven is at hand" (Mt 4:17, RSV). Peter concluded his first sermon with "Repent, and be baptized" (Acts 2:38). In the last book of the Bible the message to the seventh church is "be zealous and repent" (Rev 3:19, RSV).

Repentance is not an emotion. It is not feeling sorry for your sins. It is a decision. It is deciding that you have been wrong in supposing that you could manage your own life and be your own god; it is deciding that you were wrong in thinking that you had, or could get, the strength, education and training to make it on your own; it is deciding that you have been told a pack of lies about yourself and your neighbors and your world. And it is deciding that God in Jesus Christ is telling you the truth. Repentance is a realization that what God wants from you and what you want from God are not going to be achieved by doing the same old things, thinking the same old thoughts. Repentance is a decision to follow Jesus Christ and become his pilgrim in the path of peace.

Repentance is the most practical of all words and the most practical of all acts. It is a feet-on-the-ground kind of word. It puts a person in touch with the reality that God creates. Elie Wiesel, referring to the

It is helpful for everyone to read the Devotional and Scripture Readings and do the My Life with God Exercise before the meeting. Begin the meeting with silent prayer, then move directly to Reflecting on My Life With God below.

stories of the Hasidim, says that in the tales by Israel of Rizhim one motif recurs again and again: A traveler loses his way in the forest; it is dark and he is afraid. Danger lurks behind every tree. A storm shatters the silence. The fool looks at the lightning, the wise man at the road that lies—illuminated—before him.*

Whenever we say no to one way of life that we have long been used to, there is pain. But when the way of life is in fact a way of death, a way of war, the quicker we leave it the better. There is a condition that sometimes develops in our bodies called adhesions—parts of our internal organs become attached to other parts. The condition has to be corrected by a surgical procedure—a decisive intervention. The procedure hurts, but the results are healthy. As the Jerusalem Bible puts [Psalm 120] verses 3–4, "How will he [God] pay back the false oath / of a faithless tongue? / With war arrows hardened / over red-hot charcoal!" Emily Dickinson's spare sentence is an epigraph: "Renunciation—the piercing virtue!"

God's arrows are judgments aimed at provoking repentance. The pain of judgment called down against evil-doers could turn them also from their deceitful and violent ways to join our pilgrim on the way to peace. Any hurt is worth it that puts us on the path of peace, setting us free for the pursuit, in Christ, of eternal life. It is the action that follows the realization that history is not a blind alley, guilt not an abyss. It is the discovery that there is always a way that leads out of distress—a way that begins in repentance, or turning to God. Whenever we find God's people living in distress, there is always someone who provides this hope-charged word, showing the reality of a different day: "On that day there will be a highway all the way from Egypt to Assyria: Assyrians will have free range in Egypt, and Egyptians in Assyria. No longer rivals, they'll worship together, Egyptians and Assyrians" (Is 19:23). All Israel knew of Assyria was war—the vision shows them at worship. Repentance is the catalytic agent for the change. Dismay is transformed into what a later prophet would describe as gospel.[1]

MY LIFE WITH GOD EXERCISE

Eugene Peterson's explanation of repentance differs from a widely held concept of repentance as a more emotional experience, involving people

* Elie Wiesel, *Souls on Fire* (New York: Vintage, 1973), 154.

beating and berating themselves, weeping and moaning as they plead for God to forgive their sins. In contrast, Peterson says repentance is not an emotion or simply feeling sorry for our sins: "Repentance is a decision to follow Jesus Christ and become his pilgrim in the path of peace." Peterson's approach relies on our ability to look around our world and determine that we don't want to be a part of its lies and deception, that we want to become a disciple of Jesus Christ. Though Peterson's examples address those who have not yet put their faith in Jesus Christ, believers, too, find themselves enmeshed in the lies of the world. The need to repent of our acceptance of those ways that are not God's ways is constant. After God refuted Job's argument that he hadn't done anything wrong, Job exclaimed, "Therefore I despise myself, and repent in dust and ashes" (42:6).

It may be difficult, but we suggest you follow Peterson's advice. Look around your world. What have you incorporated into your life that is a lie? Some of the lies are so deeply embedded that they are hard to recognize, but paying attention to the magazines, TV, advertisements, and words around us can help us see some of the lies others tell us, the lies we tell ourselves. *I'm worthless. Everyone uses four-letter words. I can make it on my own. Playing violent video games or watching trash TV doesn't hurt anything. I have a right to do whatever I want. Pornography is entertainment. Greed is good. Nothing is more important than youth and beauty. If you don't do what I want, I won't love you. Your duty as my spouse is to make me happy. Men are better than women. Promiscuity isn't wrong; everyone is doing it. I have to do it my way.* The list of the world's lies is endless.

Now, do what St. Ignatius of Loyola termed an "examination of conscience," but instead of naming a fault or virtue you find in yourself and focusing on it for a half-day, determine one lie of the world you have bought into. It can be any of the above or something else you have been struggling to overcome. You might want to take a walk while you are doing the examination of conscience, or find a quiet place. Ask God to help you determine the lie that you want to renounce. Write the lie down in the margin of this book or anyplace else you see often: bathroom mirror, appointment book, and so on. Now—and this is the hardest part, the part that will require the help of the Holy Spirit—make a firm decision to quit believing this lie and turn away from it. Don't be hesitant about asking God to help you make this change in your life; all of us need help. A good way to bring this reality into your body is to turn 180 degrees from the lie every time you see or hear it. Another way is to write the lie on a piece of paper and burn it or attach it to a rock and throw it into a lake. Pay close attention to your feelings as you are doing this exercise.

REFLECTING ON MY LIFE WITH GOD
Allow each member a few moments to answer this question.

How challenging did you find it to identify and then renounce the lie? What kind of emotions did the exercise raise?

▶ **SCRIPTURE READING:** PSALM 51:1–12

After everyone has had a chance to respond to the question, ask a member to read this passage from Scripture.

Have mercy on me, O God,
    according to your steadfast love;
according to your abundant mercy
    blot out my transgressions.
Wash me thoroughly from my iniquity,
    and cleanse me from my sin.

For I know my transgressions,
    and my sin is ever before me.
Against you, you alone, have I sinned,
    and done what is evil in your sight,
so that you are justified in your sentence
    and blameless when you pass judgment.
Indeed, I was born guilty,
    a sinner when my mother conceived me.

You desire truth in the inward being;
    therefore teach me wisdom in my secret heart.
Purge me with hyssop, and I shall be clean;
    wash me, and I shall be whiter than snow.
Let me hear joy and gladness;
    let the bones that you have crushed rejoice.
Hide your face from my sins,
    and blot out all my iniquities.

Create in me a clean heart, O God,
    and put a new and right spirit within me.
Do not cast me away from your presence,
    and do not take your holy spirit from me.
Restore to me the joy of your salvation,
    and sustain in me a willing spirit.

What emotion or emotions does the psalm express? What line resonates the most with you, and why?

REFLECTION QUESTION
Allow each person a few moments to respond to this question.

▶▶ GETTING THE PICTURE

🖝 After a brief discussion, choose one person to read this section.

Psalm 51 is classified as a Penitential Psalm, along with 6, 32, 38, 102, 130, and 143. It is attributed to King David after the prophet Nathan confronted him over his affair with Bathsheba and the subsequent conspiracy to have her husband, Uriah the Hittite, killed. Despite being born the youngest son of the least family of the smallest tribe of Israel, David was anointed by God as the leader of the nation. After David's death, God praised his heart of integrity and uprightness (1 Kings 9:4), but the way David manipulated the events surrounding the seduction of Bathsheba and the death of Uriah shows that at this time David had bought into the worldly lies claiming the primacy of money, sex, and power.

Howard Macy describes Psalm 51 as "a song of repentance with a moving appeal to God's steadfast love and mercy."[2] We see an instructive progression in the psalm as the psalmist moves through several stages of repentance. First, the psalmist comes before God and throws himself on God's mercy. He can hide neither from the torment in his soul nor from God. His only course of action is to prostrate himself before the Creator of the universe and become as helpless and as dependent upon God for his life as a newly born child is dependent upon its mother.

Next, the psalmist admits that he is tainted by sin and that only God can cleanse him. He underscores his need for this cleansing with not one but three images that describe what he is asking God to do: "blot out," "wash," and "cleanse." Later, the psalmist again returns to themes of being washed and then becoming clean—"I shall be clean," "wash me," and "create in me a clean heart." The psalmist is desperate. He is haunted by the taint of the sin in his life, and he also knows that he is powerless to remove this stain on his own. He has made a decision to turn away from the sin in his life, but in order to restore his relationship with God he must humble himself and depend on God to be merciful.

The following stanza, which begins "For I know my transgressions...," contains the psalmist's confession of sin. This is no pity party. It is a realistic acknowledgment that sin has disrupted not only his own life but his relationship with God. He has bought into the lie and is paying for it. The sin *is* evil—notice the present tense—and the psalmist is prepared for and accepts any penalty God metes out: banishment from God's presence, punishment, death, whatever God deems necessary (see 2 Sam 12:9).

The psalmist is so overwhelmed by his sin that he insists he was "born guilty" and that God knew about the evil that was hatched in his heart and mind even before hearing his confession. Once he has confessed, he offers a prayer for cleansing and spiritual renewal, beginning "Create in me a clean heart. . . ." The psalmist asks God to forgive him so that he can be happy again; he petitions God to forget his sin and renovate his inner being and presses God to stay in the relationship and restore the joy he had as his child. He knows that without God he is powerless to turn away from the disposition to sin, to avoid the lie the next time around.

▶▶▶ GOING DEEPER

✍ Have another member read this section.

The psalmist knew that his sin was a form of rebellion against God, and he was afraid that God would cast him away. The Christian revelation, received through the work of Jesus Christ and the Holy Spirit, helps us understand that God does not leave us; we leave him. When we sin, we grieve the Holy Spirit (Eph 4:30), but all three expressions of God—Father, Son, and Holy Spirit—wait patiently for us to repent of our rebellion and sin and come back into fellowship with them.

Although it is never too late to repent, the longer we continue to live in our lies, the more grief will come into our lives. For the psalmist, nothing could be more clear. He put off repenting until he was overpowered by remorse and guilt. We have only to look around us to see the dysfunction caused by people who will not turn away from their sin. Unrepented sin is a cancer that eats away at us and causes great grief not only to ourselves and God but to those around us. For example, David felt the full brunt of his sin when the child he had fathered with Bathsheba died, and his family suffered from the consequences of his sin from that time on.

In his heart the psalmist knew the answer to Job's question: "Who can bring a clean thing out of an unclean? No one can" (14:4). That is why the psalmist asked God to cleanse him. He knew that he could not cleanse himself; only God could make him "whiter than snow" (Ps 51:7b). He didn't go as far as the apostle Paul does in Romans 7:18—"For I know that nothing good dwells within me, that is, in my flesh"—but admitted that he lived under the universal curse of sin. In the spiritual life there must be a constant turning *from* false assumptions, *from* skewed points of view, *from* the notion that we are totally self-sufficient, *from* our destructive lifestyles, and a turning *to* the Lord.

From the psalmist's poem we learn that sin is serious; it is not to be taken lightly. A. A. Anderson writes, "For the writer [of Psalm 51] sin is not a passing shadow but a deeply ingrained stain," a stain that can be removed only by God.[3] The psalmist found that he was enslaved to an ingrained habit of sin, and that it had worked its way out through his body (Rom 7:5). Whatever he was guilty of, whatever lie of the world he had accepted—adultery, murder, lust, envy—he had to turn away from it and start to do those things (the Spiritual Disciplines, such as prayer, worship, service, confession) that would gradually work into him in-grained patterns of righteousness.

How have you experienced repentance? Has it felt as though sin was washed or cleansed from your life?

REFLECTION QUESTION
Allow each person a few moments to respond.

▶▶▶▶ POINTING TO GOD

✍ Choose one member to read this section.

Fanny Crosby, the great American nineteenth-century hymn writer, brought many people to repentance with the more than nine thousand hymns she wrote. An illness took Frances Jane Crosby's eyesight when she was only six weeks old, but as her family read to the growing child from the Bible, they soon realized that little Fanny had an amazing memory. It was said that she could recite the first four books of both the New and Old Testaments by the time she was ten. She also had a talent for writing po-etry and as a young woman was named the Poet Laureate of the New York Institute of the Blind, the school where she had studied. In this position she met many influential people of the time, including Henry Clay, Horace Greeley, William Cullen Bryant, and President James K. Polk.

It wasn't until 1864, when she was already a published poet of note, that she tried her hand at her first hymn. Together with renowned hymn composer W. B. Bradbury she wrote these lines:

> We are going, we are going,
> To a home beyond the skies,
> Where the fields are robed in beauty
> And the sunlight never dies.

From that point on, hymn-writing became one of Crosby's central pre-occupations, as she collaborated with many others to produce thousands of hymns. She came to believe that her blindness was actually an aid to her incredible writing gift: "It seemed intended by the blessed providence of God that I should be blind all my life, and I thank him for the dispensation. If perfect earthly sight were offered me tomorrow I would not accept it. I might not have sung hymns to the praise of God if I had been distracted by the beautiful and interesting things about me."[4] Indeed, one of her most famous hymns, "Give Me Jesus," centers around the superiority of Jesus to the attractions of the world:

> Take the world, but give me Jesus,
> All its joys are but a name;
> But His love abideth ever,
> Thru eternal years the same.
>
> [Refrain]
> O the height and depth of mercy!
> O the length and breadth of love!
> O the fullness of redemption,
> Pledge of endless life above!
>
> Take the world, but give me Jesus,
> Sweetest comfort of my soul;
> With my Savior watching o'er me,
> I can sing tho billows roll.
> [Refrain]
>
> Take the world, but give me Jesus,
> Let me view His constant smile;
> Then thruout my pilgrim journey
> Light will cheer me all the while.
> [Refrain]
>
> Take the world, but give me Jesus.
> In His cross my trust shall be:
> Till, with clearer, brighter vision,
> Face to face my Lord I see.[5]
> [Refrain]

▶▶▶▶ GOING FORWARD

Have another person read this section.

Her hymn makes clear that Fanny Crosby, too, saw the value of the truth that is in Christ, in comparison to the paltry lies of the world. One of the most insidious lies in our society is the one Eugene Peterson identifies in the Devotional Reading—the lie that if we have enough money, enough education, enough friends, contacts, and success, we can make it on our own. Even those of us who have committed our lives to Christ are still vulnerable to this lie, as well as so many others. The truth is that when we try to go it alone, to serve our own interests and rely on no one but ourselves, we *will* fall into sin, and as the psalmist realized, with no small amount of difficulty, God is the only one who can cleanse us from the pain, the harm, the mark of this sin, and restore us into right relationship with him.

Repenting at its root is turning—turning from one way of life to another. As Peterson and the psalmist acknowledge, this process of turning can be painful. Yet putting off repenting will cause us more pain in the end. The decision is ours, but we have God's help with the process if we ask for it. One of the verses from Psalm 51 is a beautiful summing up of what we ask God for when we repent: "Create in me a clean heart, O God, / and put a new and right spirit within me" (v 10).

How have you seen the repercussions of delaying repentance in your own life or the life of someone around you?

REFLECTION QUESTION
Again, allow each member a few moments to answer this question.

This concludes our look at repenting. In the next chapter we will turn our attention to another avenue of prayer and worship—asking.

After everyone has had a chance to respond, the leader reads this paragraph.

Allow some time for members to encourage one another to read the Devotional and Scripture Readings and do the exercise in the following chapter before the next meeting. Then invite the members to be silent for a few moments before leading them in reading the Closing Prayer aloud together.

CLOSING PRAYER

Incline your ear, O LORD, and answer me,
    for I am poor and needy,
Preserve my life, for I am devoted to you;
    save your servant who trusts in you.
You are my God; be gracious to me, O Lord,
    for to you do I cry all day long.
Gladden the soul of your servant,
    for to you, O Lord, I lift up my soul.
For you, O Lord, are good and forgiving,
    abounding in steadfast love to all who call on you.
Give ear, O LORD, to my prayer;
    listen to my cry of supplication.
In the day of my trouble I call on you,
    for you will answer me.

At the end of the Closing Prayer, the leader asks for a volunteer to lead the next meeting.

For you are great and do wondrous things;
>> you alone are God.
Teach me your way, O LORD,
>> that I may walk in your truth. (PS 86:1–7, 10–11a)

TAKING IT FURTHER

ADDITIONAL EXERCISE

Continue your process of repenting for the lie you renounced in this chapter's exercise (or another sin that is troubling you) by confessing it to a trusted friend or advisor. Ask that person to help you turn from your sin.

ADDITIONAL RESOURCES

Bonhoeffer, Dietrich. *Psalms: The Prayer Book of the Bible.* Minneapolis, MN: Augsburg, 1970.

Foster, Richard J. *Celebration of Discipline.* San Francisco: HarperSanFrancisco, 1998.

Foster, Richard J., and others, eds., *The Renovaré Spiritual Formation Bible.* San Francisco: HarperSanFrancisco, 2005.

Peterson, Eugene H. *A Long Obedience in the Same Direction.* Downers Grove, IL: InterVarsity, 1980.

ADDITIONAL REFLECTION QUESTIONS

Was or is there a sin in your life, like the sin described by the psalmist, that haunts you? Is there one sin for which you must continually repent?

Do you agree with Eugene Peterson's assertion that "repentance is not an emotion ... it is a decision"? Why or why not?

Why do you think the image of repentance as washing or cleansing our souls of sin is so prevalent? Is the image powerful for you? Explain.

4 ASKING

DEVOTIONAL READING

AGNES SANFORD, *The Healing Light*

If we try turning on an electric iron and it does not work, we look to the wiring of the iron, the cord, or the house. We do not stand in dismay before the iron and cry, "Oh, electricity, *please* come into my iron and make it work!" We realize that while the whole world is full of that mysterious power we call electricity, only the amount that flows through the wiring of the iron will make the iron work for us.

The same principle is true of the creative energy of God. The whole universe is full of it, but only the amount of it that flows through our own beings will work for us.

We have tried often to make this creative power flow through us, saying, "Oh, God, please do this or that!" And He has not done this or that, so we have concluded that there is no use in prayer, because God, if there is such a Being, will do as He likes regardless of our wishes. In other words, we doubt the *willingness* or the *ability* of God to actually produce within our lives and bodies the results that we desire. We do not doubt our own ability to come into His presence and fill ourselves with Him, but His willingness to come into us and fill us with Himself.

My baby had been ill for six weeks with abscessed ears. I prayed desperately that God would heal the child. My mind was filled with thoughts of fear and of bitterness, and these are not of God. God is love, and perfect love casts out fear. So God could not go through me to heal my baby, for there was a break in the pipeline that connected me with Him.

Nevertheless, in His great kindness He did what He could for me. He sent me one of His own ministers. The minister was a young man, ruddy-faced, clear-eyed, full of normal, healthy interest in people and in life.

> ✍ It is helpful for everyone to read the Devotional and Scripture Readings and do the My Life with God Exercise before the meeting. Begin the meeting with silent prayer, then move directly to Reflecting on My Life With God below.

"I'll go up and have a prayer with him," he said.

"I don't think that will do any good," I replied wearily. "He's only a year and a half old. He wouldn't understand."

What I really thought was, "If God doesn't answer *my* prayers, why would He answer this minister's prayers?"

"Oh, that won't matter," cried the minister, disregarding my feeble protests. He went upstairs.

Light shone in his eyes. I looked at him and saw his joyfulness, and I believed. For joy is the heavenly "O.K." on the inner life of power. No dreary, long-faced minister could have channeled God's healing to my baby, and it was the joy on the minister's face that called forth my faith. Looking on him I knew that he had been with the One who came to give us His joy, and so I knew that the baby would be well.

The minister placed his hands upon the baby's ears and said, "Now you close your eyes and go to sleep. I'm going to ask God to come into your ears and make them well, and when you wake up you'll be all right."

He did ask God exactly that, in the simplest possible way. He closed his prayer by saying, "We thank you, Heavenly Father, because we know that this is being done. Amen."

The fever-flush died out of the baby's face immediately. He turned very pale, closed his eyes and slept. When he woke, he was well. And he never again has had abscessed ears.[1]

MY LIFE WITH GOD EXERCISE

Richard Foster tells a story about the first time he sat under the tutelage of Agnes Sanford. When he told a friend about a recent experience of praying for the healing of a man with cancer and a woman with arthritis but receiving no results, his friend invited Foster to a meeting where Sanford was speaking. As Agnes began to speak in a tiny, high voice, Foster thought skeptically, "This little old lady is going to teach *me* how to pray?" In the course of the talk, however, she explained several simple principles that have stuck with Richard to this day: first, *listen* to the Lord; second, *ask;* third, *believe;* fourth, *give thanks.* Once he started practicing these principles, Foster discovered that there is also a progression in prayer. Just as a runner must start with smaller training runs before attempting a marathon, it is good to pray first for simple things like the abscessed ears of Agnes's child, then for more difficult cases like cancer and arthritis.

During the next few days, concentrate on listening to God and asking him for help in situations in which you find yourself or your family or a good friend, rather than wishing for a change or figuring that the course of things is already predetermined. Listen for the Lord's leadings, what Richard Foster terms "a rise in the heart, a compulsion to intercede, an assurance of rightness, a flow of the Spirit. This inner 'yes' is the divine authorization for you to pray for the person or situation."[2] Start with little things first—a good night's rest for a sick friend, the solution to a problem, safe travel for a friend or a family member, the location of a lost object—because when those prayers are answered, it builds your faith so that you can believe God in bigger matters. Also remember the idea of progression, starting with smaller requests. For example, if you pray for a physical problem, be sure it is something simple, such as a fever or stomach flu, unless you are already well on the way to praying for serious illnesses. With sicknesses like stomach flu, it may not be possible to alleviate all of the symptoms; you will need to pray for the person to recover quickly, much like the minister prayed for Agnes's child. And laying your hands on people who are ill always helps direct the power of God flowing through you into that person. Remember to thank God. As you do this experiment in prayer, keep a list of the things you are praying for and the results.

What are your feelings about asking God for assistance in the small and then the big matters of life? Did the exercise change the way you felt? If so, how?

REFLECTING ON MY LIFE WITH GOD
Allow each member a few moments to answer this question.

► SCRIPTURE READING: 1 KINGS 3:3–15

Solomon loved the LORD, walking in the statutes of his father David; only, he sacrificed and offered incense at the high places. The king went to Gibeon to sacrifice there, for that was the principal high place; Solomon used to offer a thousand burnt offerings on that altar. At Gibeon the LORD appeared to Solomon in a dream by night; and God said, "Ask what I should give you." And Solomon said, "You have shown great and steadfast love to your servant my father David, because he walked before you in faithfulness, in righteousness, and in uprightness of heart toward you; and you have kept for him this great and steadfast love, and have given him a son to sit on his throne today. And now, O LORD my

After everyone has had a chance to respond to the question, ask a member to read this passage from Scripture.

God, you have made your servant king in place of my father David, although I am only a little child; I do not know how to go out or come in. And your servant is in the midst of the people whom you have chosen, a great people, so numerous they cannot be numbered or counted. Give your servant therefore an understanding mind to govern your people, able to discern between good and evil; for who can govern this your great people?"

It pleased the Lord that Solomon had asked this. God said to him, "Because you have asked this, and have not asked for yourself long life or riches, or for the life of your enemies, but have asked for yourself understanding to discern what is right, I now do according to your word. Indeed I give you a wise and discerning mind; no one like you has been before you and no one like you shall arise after you. I give you also what you have not asked, both riches and honor all your life; no other king shall compare with you. If you will walk in my ways, keeping my statutes and my commandments, as your father David walked, then I will lengthen your life."

Then Solomon awoke; it had been a dream. He came to Jerusalem where he stood before the ark of the covenant of the LORD. He offered up burnt offerings and offerings of well-being, and provided a feast for all his servants.

REFLECTION QUESTION
Allow each person a few moments to respond to this question.

If you had the same chance as Solomon and could ask God for anything, what would you ask for? Why?

▶▶ GETTING THE PICTURE

✍ After a brief discussion, choose one person to read this section.

At the time of the Scripture Reading, Solomon has only recently ascended to the throne, after the death of his father, King David, and a power struggle with his brother Adonijah. He is a very young king, yet we can see that he already has his priorities in order. He loves the Lord and follows his law. His loyalty and maturity are tested in this passage when God asks him what God should give him. Solomon's response acknowledges God's role in his own life and that of his father, David, and also Solomon's youth and lack of knowledge. Solomon knows that God made him king, just as he made David king before him, and he wants to fulfill his role as best he can. Therefore he asks God for the understanding and wisdom to be a good leader of his people.

In God's response to Solomon, he makes it clear that he is granting Solomon's request because Solomon is asking for the right thing. Considering the turmoil of Solomon's ascension to the throne and the number of people he puts to death during his early days as king (see 1 Kings 1–2), we might well expect that he would ask God for the life of his enemies, increased military power, unquestioned allegiance, or further consolidation of his kingdom. Others in the Bible certainly ask God for gifts such as long life or riches or the destruction of enemies (many of the psalms reflect this last theme), but Solomon asks for wisdom, the understanding of what is right, and God lauds him for it. It seems that Solomon's request was granted in large part because he had listened first for what God most wanted for Solomon and his reign over the people of Israel.

In the Scripture Reading we see that worship and prayer are inextricably intertwined. Solomon did not ask God for wisdom out of the blue; worship and prayer were already an ingrained pattern in his life. Before he had the dream, "Solomon offered a thousand burnt offerings on that altar [at Gibeon]" (3:4b, NIV). Afterward Solomon traveled back to Jerusalem, where the ark of the covenant was housed in a tent that David had erected, and again worshiped God through sacrifices, offerings, and a feast for his court. Solomon's dream and his request to God were bracketed by worship.

▶▶▶ GOING DEEPER

God directed Solomon to ask, and Solomon obeyed. Listening to God through prayer and worship and then asking God for what we believe is in line with his will seems so simple, yet for many of us it is incredibly difficult. We have been taught to be self-sufficient; we believe we don't need to listen to anyone in order to know what to do. In asking, we admit that a situation is beyond our control. It is much easier for us to say, "I wish this, I wish that," than it is to ask God for help. We have also been taught that everything is preordained, that we cannot really change the course of things. But the Bible shows us that we can make an objective difference with our prayers. We are "God's fellow workers" (1 Cor 3:9, NKJV), and through our asking prayers we have the chance to make a positive difference in the world around us. In the Sermon on the Mount, Jesus names the asking aspect of prayer first: "Ask, and it

Have another member read this section.

will be given to you; search, and you will find; knock, and the door will be opened for you. For anyone who asks receives, and everyone who searches finds, and for everyone who knocks, the door will be opened" (Matt 7:7–8).

This Scripture passage also reveals how much motives matter when making requests of God. Solomon asked for wisdom, not so that he could feel superior or deserving, but so that he could help his subjects. God knows when we are praying with others' best interests at heart, and he will hear and answer our prayers accordingly. Richard Foster describes in *Celebration of Discipline* how he cut out and pasted together all of Jesus's teachings about prayer and was shocked at the cumulative message. For it was immediately apparent that when Jesus prayed for others he never ended with "If it be your will." Nor did the prophets and apostles. "They obviously believed that they knew what the will of God was before they prayed the prayer of faith. They were so immersed in the milieu of the Holy Spirit that when they encountered a specific situation, they knew what should be done. Their praying was so positive that it often took the form of a direct, authoritative command: 'Walk,' 'Be well,' 'Stand up.' I saw that when praying for others there was evidently no room for indecisive, half-hoping, 'If it be thy will' prayers."[3] This strength and certainty are also evident in the example of the young minister who prayed for Agnes's son. He had the same motive as Solomon: to help. If we really love people, we want the best that life can give them, and that means we will pray for them, and pray with confidence. Love gives birth to intense, personal, practical prayer for others. Who expresses it better than the apostle John? "For this is the message you have heard from the beginning, that we should love one another. . . . Little children, let us love, not in word or speech, but in truth and action" (1 John 3:11, 18). Praying for others is love in action.

REFLECTION QUESTION
Allow each person a few moments to respond.

Do you pray differently when you pray for personal matters than when you pray for others? If so, how and why?

▶▶▶ POINTING TO GOD

✍ Choose one member to read this section.

Although Solomon asked God for wisdom in a dream, today many of us ask God for blessings and gifts through prayer and song. We see this theme of asking in many of our favorite hymns, for example those of Charles Wesley, one of Christendom's best-known hymn writers.

PRAYER AND WORSHIP

In eighteenth-century Britain, Charles and his brother John, who became the founder of the Methodist movement, helped reshape the spirituality of generations of Christians. As young men, the two founded a Holy Club at Oxford, where the members engaged in systematic study of Scripture and theological texts. While John taught and preached in England and America about experiential Christianity and his wide-ranging ideas about spirituality, Charles stayed mostly in England, using his poetic talent to write some of the most beautiful hymns the church has ever known—more than six thousand of them. From "Hark! The Herald Angels Sing" to "Christ the Lord Is Risen Today," the hymns written by Wesley have earned a permanent place in the prayer and worship life of the Church. Like Solomon, he recognized that his life's work was to help other people.

One of the Scripture passages Charles Wesley counted most influential was, "Comfort, O comfort my people, says your God" (Isa 40:1). His hymn "Jesu, My Strength, My Hope" expresses many of the themes we saw in the Scripture Reading—the confidence to pray and to know that God hears and answers, the courage to ask for wisdom ("godly fear"), and the resolve to carry out God's work:

> Jesu, my strength, my hope,
>   On thee I cast my care,
> With humble confidence look up,
>   And know thou hear'st my prayer....
>   I want a sober mind,
>   A self-renouncing will ...
>   I want a godly fear,
>   A quick-discerning eye ...
>   I want a heart to pray,
>   To pray and never cease ...
>   I want a true regard,
>   A single, steady aim ...
>
>   I rest upon thy Word,
>   The promise is for me;
> My succor, and salvation, Lord,
>   Shall surely come from thee.
>   But let me still abide,
>   Nor from thy hope remove,
> Till thou my patient spirit guide
>   Into thy perfect love.[4]

✍ Have another person read this section.

Asking God can be intimidating. We may say to ourselves, "I don't have enough faith." But the Bible tells us that if we have just the faith of a mustard seed, we can move mountains (Matt 17:20). Richard Foster assures us that "usually, the courage actually to go and pray for a person is a sign of sufficient faith."[5] This wonderful gift of prayer is incredibly exhilarating—*we are co-laborers with God*—but also a matter of great responsibility—*we are co-laborers with God!* This prayer work of ours is something we learn, something we grow better at as we become more attuned to God's workings in the world, to his calls and urgings in our own lives. But by no means wait until you feel more qualified. Begin now, begin by asking for relief for your neighbor's cold, with a whispered prayer over the letter or e-mail you send to your daughter or father or friend, with a hand on the shoulder of your companion who is suffering a loss. Above all, remember that listening to God must be the beginning of all successful prayer. Solomon had to be attuned to God in prayer and worship before he could know that asking God for the wisdom to lead his people was in harmony with God's will. If we have been asking God for something for a long time and have not been answered, perhaps this is an indication that we should leave this situation alone for now or reexamine our motives. Again, listening for God must always guide us in any kind of prayer.

REFLECTION QUESTION
Again, allow each member a few moments to answer this question.

What experiences have you had with unanswered prayers? What lessons, if any, did you learn from these experiences?

✍ After everyone has had a chance to respond, the leader reads this paragraph.

✍ **Allow some time for members to encourage one another to read the Devotional and Scripture Readings and do the exercise in the following chapter before the next meeting.** Then invite the members to be silent for a few moments before leading them in reading the Closing Prayer aloud together.

This concludes our look at asking. In the next chapter we will turn our attention to another avenue of prayer and worship—pleading.

CLOSING PRAYER

Incline your ear, O Lord, and answer me,
>for I am poor and needy,
Preserve my life, for I am devoted to you;
>save your servant who trusts in you.
You are my God; be gracious to me, O Lord,
>for to you do I cry all day long.
Gladden the soul of your servant,
>for to you, O Lord, I lift up my soul.

For you, O Lord, are good and forgiving,
 abounding in steadfast love to all who call on you.
Give ear, O LORD, to my prayer;
 listen to my cry of supplication.
In the day of my trouble I call on you,
 for you will answer me.

For you are great and do wondrous things;
 you alone are God.
Teach me your way, O LORD,
 that I may walk in your truth. (PS 86:1–7, 10–11a)

At the end of the Closing Prayer, the leader asks for a volunteer to lead the next meeting.

TAKING IT FURTHER

Try carrying a small notebook around with you to use as a prayer journal. Throughout the day jot down various prayer requests—different people or situations for which you feel the urge to pray. Note: don't hesitate to pray for these things as soon as they come to mind, too. Then, at your normal prayer time, go down your list. Write down any feelings you have during and after praying for these situations or people. You will find that some items remain on your prayer list all the time (for example, the names of your immediate family), but it is certainly okay to pray for certain people or situations for just one day. You may feel drawn to pray for some things for a set period of time—a week or ten days or thirty days. If praying for something feels uncomfortable or difficult, consider removing it from your list and leaving that situation for another person's prayers. Pay attention to God's lead in the situations and people for which he is drawing you toward prayer.

ADDITIONAL EXERCISE

Buttrick, George A. *Prayer.* Nashville, TN: Abingdon-Cokesbury, 1942.
Foster, Richard J. *Prayer: Finding the Heart's True Home.* San Francisco: HarperSanFrancisco, 1992.
Hallesby, Ole. *Prayer.* Trans. Clarence J. Carlsen. Minneapolis, MN: Augsburg Fortress, 1994.
Sanford, Agnes. *The Healing Light.* Plainfield, NJ: Logos International, 1972.
Vaswig, William L. *I Prayed, He Answered.* Minneapolis, MN: Augsburg/ Fortress, 1977.

ADDITIONAL RESOURCES

Would it change the way you pray to view prayer as a responsibility you have to make a positive difference in the world? Explain.

What type of prayer do you tend to spend the most time on—thanking, asking, confessing, listening, or another? What type of prayer do you tend to incorporate the least? Why?

What are some prayers of yours that God has answered? Did you remember to thank God for these? If not, do so now.

PLEADING

KEY SCRIPTURE: Psalm 119:145–52

DEVOTIONAL READING

ALEXANDER WHYTE, *Lord Teach Us to Pray*

"Lord, teach us to pray."
LUKE 10:1

"Let us plead together."
ISA. 43:26

We all know quite well what it is to "plead together." We all plead with one another every day. We all understand the exclamation of the patriarch Job quite well—"O that one might plead for a man with God, as a man pleadeth for his neighbour." . . .

Prayer, in its most comprehensive sense embraces many states of the mind, and many movements and manifestations of the heart. But our use of the word prayer this morning will be limited to these two elements in all true prayer—petition and pleading.

Petitioning and pleading are two quite distinct things. When we make a petition, we simply ask that something shall be granted and given. Petitioning is asking; whereas pleading is arguing. When a petitioner is in dead earnest, he is not content with merely tabling his petition. He does not simply state his bare case, and then leave it to speak for itself. No. Far from that. He at once proceeds to support his case with all the reasons and arguments and appeals that he can command. His naked petition, he knows quite well, is not enough. And thus it is that, like Job, he hastens to "order his cause before God, and fill his mouth with arguments."

Now, as was to be expected, we find that Holy Scripture is full not only of petitioning but of pleading also. Especially the Psalms. Then,

It is helpful for everyone to read the Devotional and Scripture Readings and do the My Life with God Exercise before the meeting. Begin the meeting with silent prayer, then move directly to Reflecting on My Life With God below.

again, Job is an extraordinary book in many respects; but in nothing is it more extraordinary than just in its magnificent speeches of argumentation and pleading, both with God and with man.... And then, most wonderful of all, most instructive, most impressive, and most heart-consoling of all, the 17th of John is full of this same element of reasoning and pleading,— more full of reasoning and pleading, remarkable to discover, than even of petitioning. Three petitions, or at most four, are all that our Lord makes to His Father in that great audience of His. And then, all the rest of His time and strength, in that great audience, is taken up with pleadings and arguments and reasonings and appeals,— as to why His four petitions for Himself, and for His disciples, should be heard and answered.

And then, the pleas, so to call them, that are employed by the prophets and the psalmists,—and much more by our Lord Himself, are not only so many argumentative pleas; they are absolutely a whole, and an extraordinarily rich, theology in themselves. The warrants they all build upon; the justifications they all put forward; the reasons they all assign why they should be heard and answered,—all these things are a fine study in the very deepest divinity. The things in God and in themselves that all those petitioners put forward; the allegations and pretexts they advance; the refuges they run into; and the grounds they take their last stand upon, ... are an incomparable education to every practitioner of the advocate's art. And if they are indisputably all that, then much more are those inspired prayers the very best meditation and [example] to every throne-besieging sinner, and to every importuning saint. For those great suppliants plead before God, God Himself; they plead the Divine Nature and the Divine Name: they plead, and put God in remembrance of what He can do, and what He cannot do: they plead themselves, and their depraved and debilitated human nature: and, in their last resort, they plead the very greatness of their own guilt, and their desert,—if they got their desert,—to be for ever cast out of God's presence. With such extraordinary arguments as these do God's saints fill their mouths when they enter in to petition and to plead before God.[1]

MY LIFE WITH GOD EXERCISE

Nineteenth-century preacher Alexander Whyte writes that Job (particularly 16:21), the Psalms, and John 17 all contain prayers that argue with God rather than merely petition God. He explains that those who petition God, "who simply ask that something shall be granted and given," are rarely content to stop with petitioning but rather move forward into pleading or "arguing" with him. To many of us, the idea of arguing with God is distasteful, even a little shocking. Perhaps this is because we often equate arguing with anger. Whyte's definition of this pleading or arguing, however, makes no mention of anger or indeed of any emotion at all; he describes pleading as supporting one's case "with all the reasons and arguments and appeals that he can command." Whyte does not condemn pleading, or "arguing" with God, as a form of prayer. Far from it. Instead he details how we even find Jesus pleading with God in chapter 17 of the Gospel of John—offering "pleadings and arguments and reasonings and appeals,—as to why His four petitions for Himself, and for His disciples, should be heard and answered."

Pick something very specific that you are passionate about—a job for someone you know, a person you would like to see come to know Jesus, a personality conflict, a test you will be taking, a situation you will be facing this week on your job or at home, a decision you have to make. For this exercise you should pray for something that can be accomplished in a short period of time, not something that may take months or even years to resolve. And pray for that issue as passionately as you believe in it. Feel free to present reasons to God as to why he should grant your request. Also feel free to weep. In the verse preceding the one Whyte cites, Job says, "*But* mine eye poureth out *tears* unto God" (16:20b, KJV).

If you need to, before you start praying, write down the reasons God should answer your prayer. Pray about the issue the first thing when you get out of bed in the morning, several times during the day, and the last thing at night. If you wake up in the night, pray about it again. The middle of the night is sometimes our most productive time for prayer. And be sure to ask the Holy Spirit to help: "Likewise the Spirit helps us in our weakness; for we do not know how to pray as we ought, but that very Spirit intercedes with sighs too deep for words" (Rom 8:26). If you feel like you are losing your passion for this experiment, ask the Holy Spirit to sustain and enhance it. Another teaching to remember is, "The prayer of the righteous is powerful and effective. Elijah was a human being like us, and he prayed fervently that it might not rain, and for three years and six months it did not rain on the earth. Then he prayed again, and the heaven gave rain and the earth yielded its harvest" (James 5:16b–18). Throughout, try to be intentional in nurturing your passion for the matter you are praying about, because it is all too easy to become lax and indifferent if we don't see instant or fairly prompt results.

REFLECTING ON MY LIFE WITH GOD
Allow each member a few moments to answer this question.

How did your repeated prayers go? Did you find yourself losing steam or growing more energized as the week went on? Did you see any results?

➤ SCRIPTURE READING: PSALM 119:145–52

After everyone has had a chance to respond to the question, ask a member to read this passage from Scripture.

With my whole heart I cry; answer me, O LORD.
    I will keep your statutes.
I will cry to you; save me,
    that I may observe your decrees.
I rise before dawn and cry for help;
    I put my hope in your words.
My eyes are awake before each watch of the night,
    that I may meditate on your promise.
In your steadfast love hear my voice;
    O LORD, in your justice preserve my life.
Those who persecute me with evil purpose draw near;
    they are far from your law.
Yet you are near, O LORD,
    and all your commandments are true.
Long ago I learned from your decrees
    that you have established them forever.

REFLECTION QUESTION
Allow each person a few moments to respond to this question.

What in the Scripture passage strikes you as the psalmist pleading with God?

➤➤ GETTING THE PICTURE

After a brief discussion, choose one person to read this section.

The Scripture Reading is taken from Psalm 119, the longest psalm in the Bible. Since there is no attribution for Psalm 119, scholars speculate that its author might be anyone from a king to a prisoner to a teacher in a wisdom school. Along with Psalms 111 and 112, Psalm 119 is an alphabetic acrostic poem. It contains twenty-two stanzas, corresponding to the letters in the Hebrew alphabet. Each stanza contains sixteen lines and is subdivided into eight verses, all of which start with the same letter of the Hebrew alphabet. The psalmist uses eight synonyms for God's law—commandments, statutes, ordinances, decrees, words, precepts, promises, and laws.

In the verses preceding the Scripture Reading, the psalmist piles on statement after statement, petition after petition, promise after promise, contrast after contrast on a variety of subjects, with only an occasional question addressed to God (vv 82b, 84). Suddenly, in verse 145, the mood changes drastically. The psalmist begins to plead with God: "With my whole heart I cry; answer me, O LORD" (v 145a); "I cry to you; save me" (v 146a); "I rise before dawn and cry for help" (v 147a). To support each plea, he makes a promise (v 145b), gives a reason for God to grant the request (v 146b), or affirms his hope in God (v 147b). Verses 148–52 follow the same pattern: the first line of the verse contains a statement or plea, followed by a further explanation, reason, or plea in the second line. Underlying the entire stanza is love for the laws of God and respect for the place they have in the psalmist's life. Because he relies on the law to bring order into his life and keep him from doing evil, the psalmist trusts that God will respond with protection and justice.

▶▶▶ GOING DEEPER

The passionate cries of the psalmist set a wonderful example that we can follow in our own prayer life. Being passionate before God about the injustice we see, the plight of those who have no means of support, the health of our relatives, even our own welfare makes us more human and more able to empathize with our neighbor. The psalmist expressed this passion in a number of ways in verses 145 through 148, but they all include the word *cry*. The psalmist describes a person coming before God and shouting out distress, aching for God, love of the law, fear. He used his voice to tell God what was in his "whole heart" (v 149). Neither should we hesitate to express our true feelings to God.

✍ Have another member read this section.

From the psalmist's example, we learn that we should feel free to enumerate the reasons why God should answer our prayers. Many of us find this idea uncomfortable, because we fear it may seem self-serving or arrogant. But the psalmist didn't hesitate to tell God why he came into his presence. We probably feel it is all right to cite a reason for another person to get well or to get a better job. But for ourselves? That is more problematic. Perhaps we are humble, but again perhaps we are being a little dishonest. And perhaps, just perhaps, we want to keep our true motives a secret from God.

We also see here that intention is important. The psalmist's plea did not come out of nowhere. He had already established a firm foundation of following God's law, meditating upon it, and praying routinely each morning. Because of his practice and the resulting familiarity it gave him with God's nature, he was confident that what he pled for was in line with God's law. Being intentional in the disciplines in this manner helps us to know that what we are pleading for is appropriate.

Keeping in mind that God's thoughts on living are true (v 151) and that the decrees of God are eternal (v 152), we can also take comfort in knowing that we can disagree with God and plead that he might change his mind. The Scriptures give a number of examples where people ask and God seems to give in to their wishes (Gen 18:16–33; 2 Kings 20:1–11; Jonah 3:1–10). When we plead to God we are doing something similar. We are asking the impossible, hoping beyond hope, requesting that God might, even in spite of our fragility and lack of love, change the course of events from what we expect to what we want. With a heart of love and a posture of respect, we ask that God might show a greater compassion than we have yet known. We risk it all and challenge him. Love asks us to take this risk, and it can mean putting ourselves in danger of being ostracized, called a heretic, or worse. But we plead with God nonetheless. And, in the midst of our pleading, we may just find that God is nearer than we had thought.

REFLECTION QUESTION
Allow each person a few moments to respond.

What are your feelings about offering reasons to God why he should answer your petitions?

▶▶▶▶ POINTING TO GOD

✍ Choose one member to read this section.

The music that perhaps best expresses a naked appeal to God is gospel music. Although "gospel hymns" such as those penned by Fanny Crosby had been part of American church music since before the twentieth century, it was the 1920s when blues and vaudeville musician Thomas Dorsey, the son of a Baptist minister and a church organist, first combined bluesy music with sacred lyrics in the song "If You See My Savior." Churches roundly rejected the secular sound as "the devil's music." Defeated, he returned to the blues scene, but a few years later, when his wife and son died in childbirth, he composed the emotional plea "Take My Hand, Precious Lord." It became a hit and the best known of all the hundreds of songs he penned:

PRAYER AND WORSHIP

Precious Lord, take my hand,
Lead me on, help me stand;
I am tired, I am weak, I am worn;
Thru the storm, thru the night,
Lead me on to the light:
Take my hand, precious Lord,
Lead me home.

When my way grows drear,
Precious Lord, linger near;
When my life is almost gone,
Hear my cry, hear my call,
Hold my hand lest I fall,
Take my hand, precious Lord,
Lead me home.[2]

Songs such as this one began to be performed in churches, with the congregation shouting out catchphrases or even ad-libbing new lines. Meanwhile, Dorsey worked tirelessly to convince more conservative churches to accept the new style of music. After cofounding the National Convention of Gospel Choirs and Choruses in 1933 and successfully teaming with singer Mahalia Jackson, Dorsey became known as the father of gospel music. He wrote more than eight hundred gospel songs and performed around the country. Although his songs were initially played only in African-American churches, they soon spread across racial boundaries, no doubt helped by a recording of "Peace in the Valley" by a young Elvis Presley. Gospel music is no less prominent today, featuring such mainstream artists as Kirk Franklin and Yolanda Adams. Whether the lyrics express celebration and hand-clapping joy or convey a plaintive appeal to God, such as Dorsey's "Take My Hand, Precious Lord," gospel music is notable both for its stirring appeal to God and its emotional impact on the listener.

▶▶▶▶▶ GOING FORWARD

In the end, pleading with God expresses that where we are weak, he is strong. It acknowledges that he is the only one who can grant our requests. God is responsible for the passion within us, the desire in our hearts for good for the world around us, and he wants us to work together with him to further this good. He welcomes our passionate pleas, our reasons and

Have another person read this section.

appeals and justifications. As difficult as it might be for some of us, when we are honest with God and ourselves about the reasons why we think he should grant our requests, we help ourselves to see his will and to know better what is in line with it and what is not.

REFLECTION QUESTION
Again, allow each member a few moments to answer this question.

In what matters of prayer does it make sense to plead with God?

✍ After everyone has had a chance to respond, the leader reads this paragraph.

✍ **Allow some time for members to encourage one another to read the Devotional and Scripture Readings and do the exercise in the following chapter before the next meeting.** Then invite the members to be silent for a few moments before leading them in reading the Closing Prayer aloud together.

✍ At the end of the Closing Prayer, the leader asks for a volunteer to lead the next meeting.

This concludes our look at pleading. In the next chapter we will turn our attention to another avenue of prayer and worship—cursing.

CLOSING PRAYER

Incline your ear, O Lord, and answer me,
    for I am poor and needy,
Preserve my life, for I am devoted to you;
    save your servant who trusts in you.
You are my God; be gracious to me, O Lord,
    for to you do I cry all day long.
Gladden the soul of your servant,
    for to you, O Lord, I lift up my soul.
For you, O Lord, are good and forgiving,
    abounding in steadfast love to all who call on you.
Give ear, O Lord, to my prayer;
    listen to my cry of supplication.
In the day of my trouble I call on you,
    for you will answer me.

For you are great and do wondrous things;
    you alone are God.
Teach me your way, O Lord,
    that I may walk in your truth. (PS 86:1–7, 10–11a)

TAKING IT FURTHER

ADDITIONAL EXERCISE

Read John 17 and study Jesus's pleading words to his Father. What strikes you about the way he presents his petitions?

Dorsey, Thomas. *Precious Lord: The Great Gospel Songs of Thomas A. Dorsey.* Sony, 1973.

Whyte, Alexander. *Lord Teach Us to Pray* (London: Hodder & Stoughton, 1922), 79–80, available at www.ccel.org.

How do you define pleading with God? Do you agree with Whyte that it is arguing with God, rather than merely asking him for something?

What are some of the matters about which you have pleaded with God? Are they mostly personal, or do they involve others or more general issues? Do you find it easier to plead with God about yourself or about others?

*How can you nurture your passion for those issues you want to bring be-
fore God?*

CURSING

6

KEY SCRIPTURE: Psalm 7

DEVOTIONAL READING

KATHLEEN NORRIS, *Amazing Grace*

When I'm working as an artist-in-residence at parochial schools, I like to read the psalms out loud to inspire the students, who are usually not aware that the snippets they sing at Mass are among the greatest poems in the world. But I have found that when I have asked children to write their own psalms, their poems often have an emotional directness that is similar to that of the biblical psalter. They know what it's like to be small in a world designed for big people, to feel lost and abandoned. Children are frequently astonished to discover that the psalmists so freely express the more unacceptable emotions, sadness and anger, even anger at God, and that all of this is in the Bible that they hear read in church on Sunday morning.

Children who are picked on by their big brothers and sisters can be remarkably adept when it comes to writing cursing psalms, and I believe that the writing process offers them a safe haven in which to work through their desires for vengeance in a healthy way. Once a little boy wrote a poem called "The Monster Who Was Sorry." He began by admitting that he hates it when his father yells at him; his response in the poem is to throw his sister down his stairs, and then to wreck his room, and finally to wreck the whole town. The poem concludes: "Then I sit in my messy house and say to myself, 'I shouldn't have done all that.'" "My messy house" says it all: with more honesty than most adults could have mustered, the boy makes a metaphor for himself that admitted the depth of his rage and also gave him a way out. If that boy had been a novice in the fourth-century monastic desert, his elders might have told him that he was well on the way toward repentance, not such a monster after all, but only human. If the house is messy, they might have said, why not clean it up, why not make it into a place where God might wish to dwell?[1]

It is helpful for everyone to read the Devotional and Scripture Readings and do the My Life with God Exercise before the meeting. Begin the meeting with silent prayer, then move directly to Reflecting on My Life With God below.

MY LIFE WITH GOD EXERCISE

Many of us are uncomfortable with violent or vengeful feelings as openly expressed as those of the young author of "The Monster Who Was Sorry," particularly if we have taken to heart Jesus's teaching to "love your enemies and pray for those who persecute you" (Matt 5:44). Yet as Norris points out, the psalms themselves are filled with messages similar to those expressed by the young boy. Jesus's teaching to "love your enemies" seems more radical, to say the least, when we know he would have heard the cursing psalms read in the synagogue he regularly attended on Saturdays from the time of his birth. During his schooling Jesus would have read and memorized verses such as "Happy shall they be who take your little ones and dash them against the rock!" (137:9) and "Let the wicked fall into their own nets, while I alone escape" (141:10) or "Let ruin come on them unawares" (35:8a). Because of Jesus's emphasis on loving our enemies and praying for those who persecute us, these imprecatory (or cursing) psalms are problematic for us and the Church at large, especially for those who have been raised in the peace traditions of Anabaptists and Quakers.

Yet there they are, right in the middle of the Bible. The psalms are so extraordinary in part because their words seem to run the entire gamut of human emotion, from joy to lamenting to pleading to anger. Norris writes that she believes the writing process is a safe way to express the feelings of anger or desire for vengeance that all of us have at one point or another. Indeed, expressing these feelings by writing them down seemed to bring the little boy to a place where he realized that acting on these impulses would be a mistake he would regret. In both the boy's poem and the psalms we find in the Bible, the speaker rarely ends with cursing, most often concluding with expressions of praise, thanksgiving, or hope. This is because in these "cursing" passages the psalmist *always* recognizes that justice rests entirely with God, not with us, who too often act out of anger.

To better understand the depth of the Israelites' prayers for God's help in the face of opposition, read a different psalm from the following list each day for the next six days: 35, 55, 58, 69, 83, and 140. You might want to read the psalm quickly, then go back and read it again. During the second reading, think about the tone the psalmist takes. Is the psalmist pleading with God? What reasons does the psalmist give for God to take action? What do the motives of the psalmist appear to be? How does each psalm end? After reading and examining each psalm, take a few moments to reflect on whether it expresses some of your own feelings toward people who have made you angry. You might find it helpful to write down the features common to each psalm and the emotions they aroused in you. How do you "curse" others—yelling at other drivers in traffic or complaining about co-workers to your spouse or friends or allowing small irritations to get under your skin? How do you deal with these feelings?

What did you learn about the "cursing" psalms as you studied them? Do you think they are aptly named? How can you relate them to your own experience?

REFLECTING ON MY LIFE WITH GOD
Allow each member a few moments to answer this question.

▶ SCRIPTURE READING: PSALM 7

✍ After everyone has had a chance to respond to the question, ask a member to read this passage from Scripture.

O LORD my God, in you I take refuge;
  save me from all my pursuers, and deliver me,
or like a lion they will tear me apart;
  they will drag me away, with no one to rescue.

O LORD my God, if I have done this,
  if there is wrong in my hands,
if I have repaid my ally with harm
  or plundered my foe without cause,
then let the enemy pursue and overtake me,
  trample my life to the ground,
and lay my soul in the dust. *Selah.*

Rise up, O LORD, in your anger;
  lift yourself up against the fury of my enemies;
  awake, O my God; you have appointed a judgment.
Let the assembly of the peoples be gathered around you,
  and over it take your seat on high.
The LORD judges the peoples;
  judge me, O LORD, according to my righteousness
  and according to the integrity that is in me.

O let the evil of the wicked come to an end,
  but establish the righteous,
you who test the minds and hearts,
  O righteous God.

God is my shield,
> who saves the upright in heart.
God is a righteous judge,
> and a God who has indignation every day.

If one does not repent, God will whet his sword;
> he has bent and strung his bow;
he has prepared his deadly weapons,
> making his arrows fiery shafts.
See how they conceive evil,
> and are pregnant with mischief,
> and bring forth lies.
They make a pit, digging it out,
> and fall into the hole that they have made.
Their mischief returns upon their own heads,
> and on their own heads their violence descends.

I will give to the LORD the thanks due to his righteousness,
> and sing praise to the name of the LORD, the Most High.

REFLECTION QUESTION
Allow each person a few
moments to respond to
this question.

How do you react to this psalm? Could you relate to the sentiments expressed?

▶▶ GETTING THE PICTURE

After a brief discussion, choose one person to read this section.

As stated in the exercise, the cursing psalms can be confusing for the Church and for Christians, so much so that very seldom do we hear them explained in a manner that helps us understand their origins and meaning. They were born out of the experiences of the nation of Israel and its rulers as they underwent invasions by neighboring states, ridicule by foreigners and fellow countrymen, and exile. As you discovered in your reading and study, some are written from the perspective of an individual or the righteous, others from the viewpoint of the nation of Israel as a whole. One, Psalm 55, even addresses the treachery of a friend. Perhaps the best way to start looking at the cursing psalms is to look more closely at what *curse* meant in biblical times. Sigmund Mowinckel writes:

> *Curse* is the very opposite of blessing, it is blessing with a negative sign. It likewise means 'power,' though a negative, devastating and destroying power, manifesting itself in 'misconduct,' so that

the cursed one fails in everything; he is smitten by all sorts of disaster and suffers from want of all that makes life worth living; prematurely he meets with evil and sudden death, and his family and his name are obliterated from earth. A detailed description of the destiny befalling the cursed one is given in the final passage of the 'Law,' Deut. 28.15-68.... But the curse may also be considered from another angle. The blessing power of an individual and the strong blessing power of Yahweh may be turned into a cursing power against wicked enemies—may become a legitimate defence against wicked people and be made effectual through words and rites. If anybody molests Israel, or the righteous, he will be placed under the ban of Yahweh himself (Gen. 12.3). The same thing will happen to the criminal who breaks the commandments of Yahweh and trespasses against law and religion (Mal. 2.3).[2]

Mowinckel further explains that the curse had a legitimate place in the religion and rites of Israel. Many ancient peoples, including the nation of Israel, pronounced curses against wrongdoers in their midst, to break enemies' power before going to war, and against towns who refused to help "in the struggle against the enemies of Yahweh and of Israel (Jdg. 5.23)."[3] Deuteronomy 27:14–26 lists twelve infractions for which a person could be cursed. The first curses anyone who makes and worships an idol, the next ten focus on relationships within the community, and the last stresses obedience to the law. Naturally, being deeply ingrained into the culture of the Israelites, the practice of cursing enemies to break their power made its way into the psalms.

In Psalm 7 we find the psalmist, who is identified as David, falsely accused by his enemies. In his plea, which he most likely would have made in the sanctuary, he presents his case to God as a righteous judge. First he proclaims his innocence to God, saying that if he has indeed done wrong, then God should leave him to the devices of the enemy. Then he begs God to bring judgment upon his enemies. The psalmist's words draw directly on 1 Kings 8:31–32: "'If someone sins against a neighbor and is given an oath to swear, and comes and swears before your altar in this house, then hear in heaven, and act, and judge your servants, condemning the guilty by bringing their conduct on their own head, and vindicating the righteous by rewarding them according to their righteousness.'" The psalm ends in a promise to praise the Lord for the righteousness of his character.

✍ Have another member read this section.

Injustice is every bit as much a part of our world as it was of the psalmist's. And like the psalmist, we cannot ignore it. When injustice is happening to us or to those around us, the psalmist shows us what to do: take it to God. Psalms addressing injustice, such as the one in our Scripture Reading, are written so that we can easily use them to pray about our own circumstances. Bernhard W. Anderson makes this observation: "The psalmist does not talk boringly about the details of his personal situation.... [H]e does not turn introspectively to his own inner life. Rather, by using conventional language he affirms that his situation is *typical* of every man who struggles with the meaning of his life in the concrete situations of tension, hostility, and conflict. That is why these [cursing] psalms have been used down through the centuries by suppliants who cry to God out of their concrete situation. They seem to leave a blank, as it were, for the insertion of your own personal name."[4] Every person has felt anger or a desire to "curse" another person who has wronged them or someone else they care about. We are not to try to bury these feelings and pretend to God that they are not there. Instead, the psalmist teaches us to bring them to God.

"Our hate needs to be prayed, not suppressed," wrote Eugene Peterson in *Answering God.* "Hate is our emotional link with the spirituality of evil. It is the volcanic eruption of outrage when the holiness of being, ours or another's, has been violated. It is also the ugliest and most dangerous of our emotions, the hair trigger on a loaded gun. Embarrassed by the ugliness and fearful of the murderous, we commonly neither admit nor pray our hate; we deny it and suppress it. But if it is not admitted it can quickly and easily metamorphose into the evil that provokes it; and if it is not prayed we have lost an essential insight and energy in doing battle with evil."[5] For God can use these feelings of anger, even of hate, to help ignite our work for justice. Peterson continues, "Just as hurt is the usual human experience that brings us to our knees praying for help,... so hate is frequently the human experience that brings us to our feet praying for justice, catalyzing our concern for the terrible violations against life all around us."[6] In our reaction to the injustice we see around us, we have a great opportunity to heighten our sense of what God wants for the world, to engage with him in kingdom work.

But the hardest lesson of all is that ultimately justice is in God's hands, not our own. For the psalmist to trust God to make things right took great spiritual strength of character. The psalmist knew he was innocent, and the reader can sense the anger in his words about what was done to him, but he didn't conscript the military or enlist the aid of friends to correct the evils. Instead, the psalmist went to God. Several years ago a Christian leader was teaching at a major seminary when he started to face opposition from faculty members and students. They were attacking his teachings as too controversial and theologically divisive. He quietly left the institution. When asked why he didn't try to protect his reputation, he replied, "That's Jesus's job, not mine." All of us will face situations in our lives where we believe we have been persecuted or treated unfairly. Our prayer should be to have the strength to trust God to bring justice to the situation.

How well are you doing in your life at bringing your feelings of anger before God? When in your life have feelings of anger turned to praising God?

REFLECTION QUESTION
Allow each person a few moments to respond.

▶▶▶▶ POINTING TO GOD

It is interesting to note that almost all the psalms with cursing elements have been attributed to King David. David, that young boy who so improbably beat the giant Goliath and succeeded Saul to the throne, had many enemies during his life. Members of his own family tried to usurp his throne; various rivals challenged his authority throughout his long reign; people he regarded as friends betrayed him. David, of course, was not free from sin; we all know the story of the beautiful Bathsheba and the lengths to which David was willing to go to cover up his impropriety toward her.

✍ Choose one member to read this section.

Despite the grand scale on which David lived his life, in so many ways he is every person—his humble beginnings, his improbable successes, the challenges he faced, the troubles in his family, his human weakness in matters of the flesh. Perhaps that is why he was the consummate lyricist; his songs of praise and thanksgiving bring us joy, his humble songs of repentance stir us. We can even relate to the cursing elements in his songs.

Throughout David's songs he expresses his love for God, leaving us with no doubt that David loved the Lord with all his heart. He came before God with all manner of emotion: praise and celebration—"Praise the LORD! / Sing to the LORD a new song" (Ps 149:1); pleading—"Be gracious to me, O LORD, for I am languishing; / O LORD, heal me, for my bones are shaking in terror" (6:2); humble repentance—"O LORD, do not rebuke me in your anger, or discipline me with your wrath. / For your arrows have sunk into me, / and your hand has come down on me" (38:1–2); hope—"But you, O LORD, are a shield around me, / my glory, and the one who lifts up my head. / I cry aloud to the LORD, / and he answers me from his holy hill" (3:3-4); trust—"The LORD is my shepherd, I shall not want" (23:1). It is no wonder that David's songs are still recited and sung and will always be celebrated by the People of God. Who but King David has better shown us how to come before God in prayer and worship?

▶▶▶▶ GOING FORWARD

✍ Have another person read this section.

As we see from a small sampling of the vast spectrum of David's songs, a wide range of emotions is expressed in the psalms. Most of the individual songs themselves express many emotions, moving quickly and seamlessly from a lament to a word of praise to trust and at times to what we call a curse. We can learn valuable lessons from these psalms, namely that evil is real in the world and to deny this is to fool ourselves. God wants us to see the evil and suffering in the world around us, so that we can have compassion for its victims, so that we can join him in his work for justice. If the feelings initially evoked by recognizing this evil are those of hate, anger, and vengeance, then we need to be honest before God about those feelings. So to call these psalms "cursing psalms" is really a bit of a misnomer. For most of us, our understanding of a curse is wholly negative; it is wishing nothing but bad things upon a person who we believe has wronged us. As we have seen in the "cursing" passages in the Bible, these selections are really more about taking our feelings of anger and our desire for justice to God, placing all feelings and emotions trustingly in his hands and not our own.

This is why "cursing" is never the last word. Just like the little boy who wrote the psalm and realized that sitting in his wrecked house might not be so much fun after all, we can be formed by God even when we are expressing feelings of anger. We ask him to take our anger, to carry out justice his way and in his time, with our help as appropriate, trusting him always. These feelings lead to thanksgiving, repentance, praise, even love for our enemies. If we trust him, God takes away the burden of anger and vengeance. All we have left to do is praise.

PRAYER AND WORSHIP

The cursing psalms are often skipped in modern-day prayer and worship. What role might these psalms play in your spiritual life?

REFLECTION QUESTION
Again, allow each member a few moments to answer this question

This concludes our look at cursing. In the next chapter we will turn our attention to another avenue of prayer and worship—waiting.

✍ After everyone has had a chance to respond, the leader reads this paragraph.

✍ **Allow some time for members to encourage one another to read the Devotional and Scripture Readings and do the exercise in the following chapter before the next meeting.** Then invite the members to be silent for a few moments before leading them in reading the Closing Prayer aloud together.

✍ At the end of the Closing Prayer, the leader asks for a volunteer to lead the next meeting.

CLOSING PRAYER

Incline your ear, O LORD, and answer me,
    for I am poor and needy,
Preserve my life, for I am devoted to you;
    save your servant who trusts in you.
You are my God; be gracious to me, O Lord,
    for to you do I cry all day long.
Gladden the soul of your servant,
    for to you, O Lord, I lift up my soul.
For you, O Lord, are good and forgiving,
    abounding in steadfast love to all who call on you.
Give ear, O LORD, to my prayer;
    listen to my cry of supplication.
In the day of my trouble I call on you,
    for you will answer me.

For you are great and do wondrous things;
    you alone are God.
Teach me your way, O LORD,
    that I may walk in your truth. (PS 86:1–7, 10–11a)

TAKING IT FURTHER

Write your own cursing psalm. Use some of the same devices and methods utilized by the writers of the psalms you studied in the exercise and in the Scripture Reading. Feel free to express your darkest emotions to God and ask for his help in dealing with them. Use the animosity you feel toward the people who you believe have wronged you before God. When you have finished, bring all of those feelings and your poem before God and, if you believe you should confess your hatred or dislike

ADDITIONAL EXERCISE

for a person who has treated you badly, do so. Then burn the poem. As the smoke rises into the air, ask God to give you freedom from unhealthy thoughts of anger and vengeance.

ADDITIONAL RESOURCES

Anderson, Bernhard W. *Out of the Depths: The Psalms Speak for Us Today*. Philadelphia: Westminster, 1970.

Norris, Kathleen. *Amazing Grace*. New York: Riverhead, 1998.

Mowinckel, Sigmund. *The Psalms in Israel's Worship*. Grand Rapids, MI: Eerdmans, 2004.

Peterson, Eugene H. *Answering God: The Psalms as Tools for Prayer*. San Francisco: HarperSanFrancisco, 1989.

ADDITIONAL REFLECTION QUESTIONS

In your life, has writing out feelings of anger or a desire for vengeance been a healthy way to deal with such feelings? How else could you bring such feelings to God?

When have you suppressed or denied feelings of hate, anger, or vengeance toward another person? What was the result?

Bad things happening to good people is a situation with which we struggle, but when bad things happen to those we consider to be bad people, sometimes we gloat, a feeling that has no place in the with-God life. Identify a time in your life when you rejoiced in someone else's misfortune. How can you avoid such feelings in the future?

7 WAITING

DEVOTIONAL READING

LUCI SHAW, *Water My Soul*

The lesson of waiting is of vital importance to people living in our culture—the age of instant gratification. We demand instant communication (the "snail mail" of the postal service has become too frustratingly slow and unreliable for us), and we achieve it with the clever new technologies for which our half of the twentieth century is renowned—telephones, facsimile machines, electronic mail. We want instant meals, so we pop a TV dinner into the microwave, or we whip up instant mashed potatoes. Never mind that they don't taste like much; they're *fast!*

Other created beings seem to have more of an inborn capacity to wait. I've watched bald eagles on the coast of the Olympic Peninsula, floating, waiting for the rising thermals of air, needing only to tilt an edge of feathers for a new direction or greater altitude. Even the trees in autumn seem to wait for a command (inaudible to us) that tells them, "Fall!" And then, sometimes with no perceptible breath of air, the leaves begin to fill the air with their shining flecks and line the woods with gold leaf....

Those of us who are bewildered by personal tragedies ("How can this be God's will?") or who are constantly impatient for *results* (and I include myself) need to heed the words of St. John Chrysostom, that fourth-century scholar and saint. In her book *The Cloister Walk*, Kathleen Norris quotes him as describing someone with no knowledge of agriculture "observing a farm collecting grain and shutting it in a barn to protect it from the damp. Then he sees the same farmer take the same grain and cast it to the winds, spreading it on the ground, maybe even

It is helpful for everyone to read the Devotional and Scripture Readings and do the My Life with God Exercise before the meeting. Begin the meeting with silent prayer, then move directly to Reflecting on My Life With God below.

in the mud, without worrying any more about the dampness. Surely he will think that the farmer has ruined the grain, and reprove the farmer." Norris goes on: "The reproof comes from ignorance and impatience, Chrysostom says; only waiting until the end of the summer, he would see the farmer harvest the grain, and be astonished at how it has multiplied. So much the more, he adds . . . should 'we await the final outcome of events, remembering who it is who plows the earth of our souls.'"

Any skill that demands a long apprenticeship is bound to be unpopular. When I offer a poetry workshop students often show up wanting to be made into instant poets, "Just show me how, and I'll just do it." Inexperienced poets think the work is finished after a couple of drafts of a poem. They're shocked when I tell them I often revise my poems thirty, forty, fifty times over a period of months or years before the poem settles into itself and lets me know it's complete, the poem it was meant to be. It's not a matter of simply knowing the rules for poetry and employing them like a mathematical formula. It doesn't work that way. . . . The only way we learn to write is—to write and rewrite and rewrite over the years, listening to the metaphors, seeing the images, learning from ourselves and our own poems (and those of others) how language works, and trying not to shortchange either.

It's the same thing with learning to live like God, *for* God, *with* God. We won't get it right the first time. Walking, getting lost, starting over, stumbling, falling and picking ourselves up, hanging onto God's hand, listening for his instructions, learning where to place our feet, how to anticipate obstacles, allowing our muscles to toughen with exercise so that we won't fall victim to fatigue; all this training is time consuming. Maturity waits for experience to teach us. We keep hoping someone will publish a how-to book with *The Ten Easy Steps to Maximum Growth*. Wait on. And learn as you wait![1]

MY LIFE WITH GOD EXERCISE

For the next few days we are going to attempt what may sound like an oxymoron: to work on growing our souls by waiting. Somehow, in the midst of your schedule, set aside half an hour per day to wait. This can be done in a multitude of ways. Take a long soak in a bathtub. Sit quietly under a tree. Lie on a bed or grass or carpet. Sit in a rocking chair and look out the window. Turn off the TV and relax in your recliner. Before you start, dedicate this period of waiting to God. While you are waiting, listen. Listen to the birds singing. Listen to the train blowing its horn. Listen to children playing in the schoolyard. Listen to the car stopping at a stop sign. Listen to the wind rustling tree leaves. Listen to the sounds of the city coming awake. Then gradually, deliberately listen for God speaking to you as you are waiting. Remember, you are *not* doing nothing; you are making space for your soul to grow. Since this exercise focuses on waiting, feel free to temporarily put aside your journal or Bible study or whatever you regularly do to keep the communication lines between God and yourself open. If you feel you must carry through on your promises and practices of praying for other people, try to do that at another time. We might say waiting is wasting time with God, but the truth is that time spent before God is never wasted.

How did you wait? What did you learn?

REFLECTING ON MY LIFE WITH GOD
Allow each member a few moments to answer this question.

➤ SCRIPTURE READING: PSALM 130

⌇ After everyone has had a chance to respond to the question, ask a member to read this passage from Scripture.

Out of the depths I cry to you, O LORD.
    Lord, hear my voice!
Let your ears be attentive
    to the voice of my supplications!

If you, O LORD, should mark iniquities,
    Lord, who could stand?
But there is forgiveness with you,
    so that you may be revered.

I wait for the LORD, my soul waits,
    and in his word I hope;
my soul waits for the Lord
    more than those who watch for the morning,
    more than those who watch for the morning.

O Israel, hope in the LORD!
    For with the LORD there is steadfast love,
    and with him is great power to redeem.
It is he who will redeem Israel
    from all its iniquities.

REFLECTION QUESTION
Allow each person a few
moments to respond to
this question.

Why do you think the psalmist connected waiting with hope?

▶▶ GETTING THE PICTURE

✍ After a brief discus-
sion, choose one person
to read this section.

Psalm 130 is generally classified as a psalm of repentance because of its confessional nature and how it is often used within the Christian community. But it also is classified as one of the "Songs of Ascents"—the psalms that were used by pilgrims on their way to Jerusalem—and contains features of an individual lament. Psalm 130 consists of four parts, or couplets. The first three couplets alternate between two names for God—a shortened version of Yahweh, rendered "LORD," and Adonai, translated "Lord." In the Old Testament, Yahweh was the most important title or name for God. It was the Divine Name God revealed to Moses at the burning bush. The name Yahweh became so sacred that the other name for God used in this psalm, Adonai, was pronounced in its place during the postexilic period. Adonai is a "title of respect used to address a social superior (e.g., king, husband, slave owner)."[2] If we compare Psalm 130 to the psalms around it, we see that it was much more common for the psalmist to refer to God only as Yahweh. By using Adonai as well as Yahweh, the psalmist seems to emphasize the master-servant relationship between God and humankind.

The first couplet is a lament in which the psalmist cries out to God and pleads for God to hear him "out of the depths." This phrase calls to mind Jonah's prayer when he was in the belly of the fish: "Out of the belly of Sheol [the place of the dead] I cried, / and you heard my voice" (2:2b). By using a metaphor that emphasizes how greatly he is separated from God, the psalmist, like Jonah, throws himself upon God's mercy. That and the use of Adonai reinforce the view that God is the master and the psalmist is the servant.

The first two lines of the second couplet contain a confession of sin, but the psalmist speaks in generalities, not about specific sins. These lines acknowledge that the extent of the psalmist's sins cannot be measured. If God were to keep track of our sins, it would be impossible for anyone to come into the presence of God. Even though God demands sinlessness, the last two lines emphasize that he forgives, and because he forgives, God is to be given honor, another admission that this is a relationship of servant to master.

Even in his desperate state of sinfulness and suffering, the palmist still waits before the Lord and hopes in his word. The psalmist equates his waiting to that of a watchman. In ancient Israel there were two kinds of watchmen: those who kept watch over the city from the walls during the night, and the Levites, who waited for the dawn so they could offer the daily morning sacrifice. Both must have greatly anticipated and longed for the morning to come, but they needed patience to do their job well. The psalmist says that he has more patience than either kind of watchman in waiting for the Lord. He can be so patient because he has hope in the Lord. Eugene Peterson explains this hope of the psalmist: "Hoping is not dreaming. It is not spinning an illusion of fantasy to protect us from our boredom or our pain. It means a confident, alert expectation that God will do what he said he will do. . . . It is a willingness to let God do it his way and in his time."[3]

The psalmist and, indeed, all Israel can hope in the Lord because Yahweh will redeem his people—that is, restore or reestablish his relationship with Israel in spite of its sinfulness.

▶▶▶ GOING DEEPER

Psalm 130 teaches us that regardless of how low we are—mentally, physically, emotionally, or spiritually—God is with us. During World War II, the theologian Jürgen Moltmann served as a German soldier. After surrendering to the British, he spent three years in Allied prison camps. This long period of waiting in the camps weighed on Moltmann. As the Third Reich collapsed, he saw fellow German soldiers completely lose hope, sicken, and even die. He himself felt increasingly burdened by grief and guilt. Although he had no Christian background, Moltmann was given a New Testament and Psalms by an American chaplain. He read in Psalm 139, "If I make my bed in hell, behold thou art there" (v 8, KJV), and wondered if that meant God was even in the prison camp. As he read on, Moltmann became convinced that the answer was yes, that God "was present even behind barbed wire—no, most of all behind the barbed wire."[4] His long period of waiting had led to a life-altering revelation. Regardless of where we are, how we got there, whether we want to stay or leave, God is there. Psalm 139 also asks, "Where can I go from your spirit? / Or where can I flee from your presence?" (v 7).

Have another member read this section.

God is always present with us, and if we wait, God will make us aware of his presence.

The psalm teaches us that waiting is not doing nothing. It is actively watching for the Lord, just like any night watchman watches carefully over the city. It is hoping in the Lord, trusting in God's love and power of redemption. In the POW camp, Moltmann "also found something new in the Psalms: hope. Walking the perimeter of the barbed wire at night for exercise, he would circle a small hill in the center of the camp on which stood a hut that served as a chapel. That hut became for him a symbol of God's presence in the midst of suffering."[5] Because he was a prisoner, Moltmann had nothing to do except to wait. He used this time to read the Psalms and find hope. In our busyness we find all kinds of excuses for why we cannot set aside time to wait before God. Because of this, we should not be surprised that we often feel hopeless.

And last, we are to encourage others to hope in the Lord. Just as the psalmist implored his nation to hope, today we have only to look around us to see people, organizations, and institutions that are bereft of hope. In *The Divine Conspiracy,* Dallas Willard writes, "There are none in the humanly 'down' position so low that they cannot be lifted up by entering God's order, and none in the humanly 'up' position so high that they can disregard God's point of view on their lives.... The barren, the widow, the orphan, the eunuch, the alien, all models of human hopelessness, are fruitful and secure in God's care."[6] And who better to bring a message of hope to the world than those who wait on a God who has redeemed them and steadfastly loves them? In cooperation with the Holy Spirit, we have the power to proclaim this hope to a world longing to hear it. But first we have to learn to wait, for in waiting we hear and experience the hope God longs for us to share.

REFLECTION QUESTION
Allow each person a few moments to respond.

How is watching a part of waiting? How is hope a part of waiting?

▶▶▶▶ POINTING TO GOD

✍ Choose one member to read this section.

Matt Redman, one of the most popular contemporary worship leaders of our day, has written many memorable songs, including "Better Is One Day" and "Let My Words Be Few." But perhaps his best-known song is "The Heart of Worship," which has been recorded by Christian artists such as Michael W. Smith and Sonic Flood. The song came out of a powerful experience shared by Matt and his church. Matt's country of England and his church, Soul Survivor in Watford, were at the forefront of the contemporary worship revival characterized by band-led music, sound systems, and praise songs such as those published by John Wimber's Vineyard Music. But despite the increasing popularity of their music style, the pastor of Soul Survivor, Mike Pilavachi, felt that there was something wrong with their music-driven service. He worried that the members were consumers of the worship music, not active participants.

"There was a dynamic missing, so the pastor did a pretty brave thing," said Redman. "He decided to get rid of the sound system and band for a season, and we gathered together with just our voices. His point was that we'd lost our way in worship, and the way to get back to the heart would be to strip everything away."[7] Without their usual worship accompaniments, the congregation entered a season of waiting to hear what the Lord would say to them about worship. Pilavachi asked them, "When you come through the doors on a Sunday, what are you bringing as your offering to God?" At first his words were greeted with silence, but eventually the members of the church responded with prayers and a cappella singing. Challenging themselves to develop new ways to worship gave them a new understanding of what it meant to participate in worship.

Redman responded to the experience by writing "The Heart of Worship," which begins:

> When the music fades and all is stripped away
> And I simply come
> Longing just to bring something that's of worth
> That will bless Your heart
>
> I'll bring You more than a song
> For a song in itself
> Is not what You have required
> You search much deeper within
> Through the way things appear
> You're looking into my heart
>
> I'm coming back to the heart of worship
> And it's all about You
> All about You, Jesus

Although Redman wrote the song as his own personal response, he showed it to his pastor, who encouraged him to change a few words to make it applicable to everyone. The song became the centerpiece of an album Redman released and quickly became an international hit. Meanwhile, Soul Survivor Church returned to its normal worship style, with band and sound system. Their period of waiting for the Lord had borne beautiful fruit, not just in the song that has inspired Christians the world over, but in the hearts of the Soul Survivor congregation. "We'd gained a new perspective that worship is all about Jesus, and He commands a response in the depths of our souls no matter what the circumstance and setting," says Redman. "'The Heart of Worship' simply describes what occurred."[8]

>>>>>> GOING FORWARD

Have another person read this section.

All of us have seasons in our life in which we clearly recognize that we are waiting—waiting for God to help bring to fruition a vision he has given us, waiting to meet the person who will become our spouse, waiting to finish school and begin a job, waiting for a career to reach a certain pinnacle. As Christians, we are all waiting and watching for our Lord to come again to redeem the world. Our usual reaction to waiting, however, is impatience. Rarely do we recognize the waiting itself as beneficial. But Psalm 130 clearly states that waiting on the Lord is an important part of the with-God life.

Waiting teaches us that God's time is not always our own. As we read in 2 Peter, "With the Lord one day is like a thousand years, and a thousand years are like one day" (3:8). Waiting also prepares and forms us for future challenges. It is a good in and of itself. Waiting is not wasting; it is not sitting and doing nothing. It has a very clear purpose. Waiting is a time for us to develop hope in the Lord, to reflect on who he is and what he has done and will in the future do in our lives, to watch and listen attentively for him. It is the time in which we surrender: "Your will, Lord, not my own." If we learn to wait and hope in the Lord, truly we follow Jesus's direction in John 15:5: "Those who abide in me and I in them bear much fruit."

REFLECTION QUESTION
Again, allow each member a few moments to answer this question.

When in your life have you been most conscious of waiting? What was your reaction to this feeling?

PRAYER AND WORSHIP

This concludes our look at waiting. In the next chapter we will turn our attention to another avenue of prayer and worship—lamenting.

CLOSING PRAYER

Incline your ear, O Lord, and answer me,
　　for I am poor and needy,
Preserve my life, for I am devoted to you;
　　save your servant who trusts in you.
You are my God; be gracious to me, O Lord,
　　for to you do I cry all day long.
Gladden the soul of your servant,
　　for to you, O Lord, I lift up my soul.
For you, O Lord, are good and forgiving,
　　abounding in steadfast love to all who call on you.
Give ear, O Lord, to my prayer;
　　listen to my cry of supplication.
In the day of my trouble I call on you,
　　for you will answer me.

For you are great and do wondrous things;
　　you alone are God.
Teach me your way, O Lord,
　　that I may walk in your truth. (PS 86:1–7, 10–11a)

✍ After everyone has had a chance to respond, the leader reads this paragraph.

✍ **Allow some time for members to encourage one another to read the Devotional and Scripture Readings and do the exercise in the following chapter before the next meeting.** Then invite the members to be silent for a few moments before leading them in reading the Closing Prayer aloud together.

✍ At the end of the Closing Prayer, the leader asks for a volunteer to lead the next meeting.

TAKING IT FURTHER

Silence is a Spiritual Discipline that can be closely tied to waiting. Consider adding a period of silence to your prayer practice. For a certain period of time each day or each week, sit in silence and wait upon the Lord.

ADDITIONAL EXERCISE

ADDITIONAL RESOURCES

Peterson, Eugene H. *A Long Obedience in the Same Direction*. Downers Grove, IL: InterVarsity, 1980.
Redman, Matt. *The Unquenchable Worshipper: Coming Back to the Heart of Worship*. Ventura, CA: Regal, 2001.
Shaw, Luci. *Water My Soul*. Grand Rapids, MI: Zondervan, 1998.

What is your usual attitude toward waiting? When are you the most impatient?

Look back on a time in your life when you were waiting for something specific. How did you feel about the waiting at the time? Now, with hindsight, how do you view that period of waiting? Was God using the waiting to prepare you? Think about the role waiting plays in your life now. Would it be helpful to deliberately set aside in your schedule some time for waiting, for deliberately wasting time with God?

How do you feel about waiting for Jesus to come again?

LAMENTING

KEY SCRIPTURE: Psalm 22:1–11, 19–24

DEVOTIONAL READING

NICHOLAS WOLTERSTORFF, *Lament for a Son*

I walked into a store. The ordinariness of what I saw repelled me: people putting onions into baskets, squeezing melons, hoisting gallons of milk, clerks ringing up sales. "How are you today?" "Have a good day now." How could everybody be going about their ordinary business when these were no longer ordinary times? I went to my office and along the way saw the secretaries all at their desks and the students all in their seats and the teachers all at their podiums. Do you not know that he slipped and fell and that we sealed him in a box and covered it with dirt and that he can't get out?

I have been daily grateful for the friend who remarked that grief isolates. He did not mean only that I, grieving, am isolated from you, happy. He meant also that *shared* grief isolates the sharers from each other. Though united in that we are grieving, we grieve differently. As each death has its own character, so too each grief over a death has its own character—its own inscape. The dynamics of each person's sorrow must be allowed to work themselves out without judgment. I may find it strange that you should be tearful today but dry-eyed yesterday when my tears were yesterday. But my sorrow is not your sorrow.

There's something more: I must struggle so hard to regain life that I cannot reach out to you. Nor you to me. The one not grieving must touch us both. It's when people are happy that they say, "Let's get together."

What is it that makes the death of a child so indescribably painful? I buried my father and that was hard. But nothing at all like this. One expects to bury one's parents; one doesn't expect—not in our day and age—to bury one's children. The burial of one's child is a wrenching alteration of expectations.

☞ It is helpful for everyone to read the Devotional and Scripture Readings and do the My Life with God Exercise before the meeting. Begin the meeting with silent prayer, then move directly to Reflecting on My Life With God below.

But it's more than that. I feel the more but cannot speak it. A child comes into the world weak and vulnerable. From the first minutes of life, we protect it. It comes into the world without means of sustenance. Immediately we the parents give of our own. It begins to display feelings and thoughts and choices of its own. We celebrate those and out of our own way of being-in-the-world try to shape and direct and guide them. We give of ourselves to the formation of this other, from helplessness to independence, trying our best to match our mode of giving to the maturing of the child—our giving maturing with the child's maturing. We take it on ourselves to stay with this helpless infant all the way so that it has a future, a future in which we can delight in its delight and sorrow in its sorrow. Our plans and hopes and fears are plans and hopes and fears for it. Along the way we experience the delights and disappointments of watching a future take shape, from babblings to oratory, from flounderings to climbing, from dependence to equality.

And now he's gone. That future which I embraced to myself has been destroyed. He slipped out of my arms. For twenty-five years I guarded and sustained and encouraged him with these hands of mine, helping him to grow and become a man of his own. Then he slipped out and was smashed.[1]

MY LIFE WITH GOD EXERCISE

Nothing is harder emotionally on parents than the death of a child. Many times those who have lost a child never recover from the resulting wound in their souls. As Wolterstorff explains, unexpected tragedies like his son's death in a rock-climbing accident are all the harder because we never anticipate such a crisis. Making matters worse, there is very little space for mourning in our culture. We no longer as a matter of course wear an outward sign of our suffering, such as black clothing, veils, or armbands. We don't sit shiva like Orthodox Jews, or spend a prescribed number of days wailing, as is still the custom in many cultures around the world. We are instead expected to put our grief aside and go on with the world as usual, even when we are so rocked by grief that the world no longer seems the same place it once was. This kind of expectation can be crazy-making. Indeed, although modern psychology tells us that we must not ignore our grief, society pressures us to do just that.

Nicholas Wolterstorff was able to give voice to his pain by writing *Lament for a Son*, although surely it could not fully heal the wound of his grieving. In this exercise, we ask you to search your life for a loss over which you did not fully grieve. It may be an obvious tragedy, one that you are consciously struggling with even now, or it may be something that happened in the past. It does not have to be the death of a loved one. Perhaps it was the loss of a cherished relationship, a job, or a part of your body through disease or accident—anything that caused you great pain. Whatever you have lost, you need not revisit all the details, but try to create a space for healing, so that the wound may continue to lose its rawness. Go to a person you trust and talk about it. Write a letter to your best friend or to God in which you explain your feelings, then store it in a safe place. Go somewhere secluded where you can talk with God about how much you are hurting; get angry and shout if necessary. If you have already done these things, seek out a person who can pray with you and for you.

This first part of the exercise might be quite enough for you, but if you feel that there has been no great loss in your life for which you need to spend more time grieving or if you work through the first part of the exercise and would like to move on, the second part of the exercise centers around Wolterstorff's statement, "The one not grieving must touch us." For this part of the exercise, visit (or call) someone you know who is in the throes of grief. Be sure to call ahead to make sure your visit is all right. As you are visiting, be sensitive to their demeanor. Do they seem too cheerful? Full of clichés? Talkative? Any of these exteriors can hide a person's true feelings. If you are able to visit in person, be aware of your surroundings. Is the house messy or dirty? Does their outward appearance indicate neglect? These signs could indicate depression. Try to listen instead of talking, so that you discover things you can do to help them: clean house, run errands, provide a ride, or cook a meal. When talking, avoid clichés like "It was God's will," "You'll see them again in heaven," "Maybe it was time for him or her to leave us," or "You'll get over it." At the end of your visit ask if it would be all right to pray for them. Be sure to listen for and heed the promptings of the Holy Spirit as you talk with the person and pray. If it seems right, ask if they would mind if you visited again.

What did you learn about grieving?

> ## SCRIPTURE READING: PSALM 22:1–11, 19–24

My God, my God, why have you forsaken me?
    Why are you so far from helping me, from the words of
    my groaning?

REFLECTING ON MY LIFE WITH GOD
Allow each member a few moments to answer this question.

↪ After everyone has had a chance to respond to the question, ask a member to read this passage from Scripture.

O my God, I cry by day, but you do not answer;
>   and by night, but find no rest.

Yet you are holy,
>   enthroned on the praises of Israel.
In you our ancestors trusted;
>   they trusted, and you delivered them.
To you they cried, and were saved;
>   in you they trusted, and were not put to shame.

But I am a worm, and not human;
>   scorned by others, and despised by the people.
All who see me mock at me;
>   they make mouths at me, they shake their heads;
"Commit your cause to the LORD; let him deliver—
>   let him rescue the one in whom he delights!"

Yet it was you who took me from the womb;
>   you kept me safe on my mother's breast.
On you I was cast from my birth,
>   and since my mother bore me you have been my God.
Do not be far from me,
>   for trouble is near
>   and there is no one to help....

But you, O LORD, do not be far away!
>   O my help, come quickly to my aid!
Deliver my soul from the sword,
>   my life from the power of the dog!
Save me from the mouth of the lion!

From the horns of the wild oxen you have rescued me.
I will tell of your name to my brothers and sisters;
>   in the midst of the congregation I will praise you:
You who fear the LORD, praise him!
>   All you offspring of Jacob, glorify him;
>   stand in awe of him, all you offspring of Israel!
For he did not despise or abhor
>   the affliction of the afflicted;
he did not hide his face from me,
>   but heard when I cried to him.

What emotions in the psalm struck you the most?

REFLECTION QUESTION
Allow each person a few moments to respond to this question.

▶▶ GETTING THE PICTURE

Unlike our culture in the twenty-first-century Western world, the Israelites had recognizable customs centering around mourning. Outward displays of grief were acceptable; we read in the Bible of public weeping and people clothing themselves in sackcloth and ashes. Even Spiritual Disciplines, such as fasting and prayer, were often a public part of lamenting. This type of grieving might follow the death of a loved one, but often it was the practice of the entire community or a group within that community to mourn a terrible happening; for example, in Esther 4:3, after Mordecai learns that King Ahasuerus has signed an edict ordering that all the Jews be put to death on a certain day, "in every province, wherever the king's command and his decree came, there was great mourning among the Jews, with fasting and weeping and lamenting, and most of them lay in sackcloth and ashes." The community also cried together in worship settings for help from God; this is the context from which lament psalms such as Psalm 22 evolved. These psalms would have been recited publicly.

↪ After a brief discussion, choose one person to read this section.

Just as it seemed that Wolterstorff found solace in writing his lament for his son, so psalmists and worshiping communities alike dealt with crisis and their resulting feelings of mourning, grief, and abandonment by writing and reciting psalms of lament. Psalm 22 is commonly characterized as an individual or personal lament psalm. The psalmist starts the poem with a question many of us have heard as one of Jesus's last statements on the cross, "My God, my God, why have you forsaken me?" (Matt 27:46). The repetition of God's name emphasizes the depth of the poet's suffering and despair, but the use of the personal pronoun ("my God") creates a picture of intimacy with God, what A. A. Anderson describes as a "bridge between utter despair and hope."[2] Indeed, we see the psalmist shift from despair to hope as we move from the first stanza to the second. The psalmist is despondent because he receives no answer from God during his waking hours and cannot sleep at night, but in the second stanza he starts to reassure himself that God will alleviate his suffering because he delivered Israel.

The construction of the first two stanzas of Psalm 22 contrasts the psalmist's suffering with the deliverance of Israel. The words of the second stanza almost seem to provide answers to the despairing questions of the first stanza. It is clear that the psalmist is contrasting his present state with what happened to his nation, and is appealing to God to help him for the same reason he helped Israel, because God is his God and he trusts in him, just as God was Israel's God and they trusted in him.

In the second-to-last stanza, the psalmist pleads with God to come quickly to help. He uses four metaphors for the evil that surrounds him: a sword, a dog, a lion, and wild oxen, all of which speak of violent death. But in the last stanza, we see that God rescues him from this terrible, demeaning fate. The lament moves into praise and thanksgiving. It also gives us a glimpse of how such psalms were used in worship. While this particular lament psalm tells of individual woes rather than community troubles, the psalmist makes it clear that the community is involved in his lament and in the thanks he offers when God answers his call. The psalmist speaks of telling his brothers and sisters about God, of praising in "the midst of the congregation" (v 22). The psalm goes on to describe a shared meal in honor of the psalmist's deliverance (v 26). While his lament may have made the psalmist feel alone, he soon returned to the arms of his community.

▶▶▶ GOING DEEPER

✒ Have another member read this section.

The Devotional and Scripture Readings give us a clear view of the suffering and despair that we as human beings undergo during our journey through life. Wolterstorff's essay vibrates with grief and sorrow, while the psalmist's poem initially exudes despair but moves toward hope and assurance. The psalm reflects a trust in God that can overcome all obstacles, even death. In fact, the last stanza of the psalm alludes to the resurrection of everyone who has ever lived: "To [God], indeed, shall all who sleep in the earth bow down; / before him shall bow all who go down to the dust, / and I shall live with him" (v 29). This complete and utter faith in God is at the heart of all of the psalms, even the psalms of lament.

Both readings point to the fact that we have no control over many things that happen to us or to others. A drunk driver loses control and slams into our car. We contract cancer or a life-threatening virus. Fire breaks out in the hotel where we are staying. A downturn in the economy forces our supervisor to fire us. All are beyond our control. Like the psalmist, we demand an answer from God, but many times no answer comes. The important thing is to keep bringing our prayers and laments before God. We do not know what exactly has happened to make the psalmist lament so mournfully. Indeed, as we saw in the chapter about the cursing psalms, the very vagueness of the psalm enables us to easily see ourselves in the psalmist's place, to insert our own troubles into his lament. His troubles become ours, his enemies our own, and we can call out to God with him. And this is what God calls us to do: to take our grief, confusion, and mourning to him.

The psalm also reveals that our suffering, painful though it may be, is temporary. "The laments are almost unanimously moving toward resolution of the crisis at hand," writes Bellinger.[3] Because God is holy, he rescued the nation of Israel from bondage in Egypt after they cried out to him and trusted him. Though the psalmist despaired and suffered mightily for an undetermined amount of time, God rescued him from the people who wanted to kill him. The apostle Paul's teaching reinforces the earlier view of the psalmist: "For this slight momentary affliction is preparing us for an eternal weight of glory beyond all measure, because we look not at what can be seen; for what can be seen is temporary, but what cannot be seen is eternal" (2 Cor 4:17–18).

How has your faith in God brought you through difficult times in your life?

REFLECTION QUESTION
Allow each person a few moments to respond.

▶▶▶▶ POINTING TO GOD

Eighteenth-century British hymn writer Anne Steele knew what it was to lament and mourn. She lost her mother when she was three years old, at nineteen she suffered a debilitating hip injury that left her an invalid, and at twenty-one she lost her fiancé to a drowning accident the day before their wedding. Like Wolterstorff and the psalmist, Steele seems to have dealt with the tragedies by writing. Over her lifetime, she wrote volumes of devotional poetry and 144 hymns, while assisting her father in his part-time pastoral work in the Baptist Church despite her frailty. Her hymns became extremely popular. In 1914, Amos Wells wrote that she was "the first woman writer whose hymns came to be largely used in hymn-books, and she is the greatest Baptist hymn-writer."[4] In *Baptist Hymn Writers and Their Hymns,* Henry Burrage wrote that "her hymns, written to lighten her own burdens, give beautiful expression to the sweetness of her Christian character, and the depth of her Christian experience." Perhaps nowhere is this better expressed than in the hymn she wrote upon hearing the news of her fiancé's death. From its moving words, it is evident that she was able to bring her laments before God and receive solace from him:

✒ Choose one member to read this section.

When I survey life's varied scene
Amid the darkest hours
Sweet rays of comfort shine between
And thorns are mixed with flowers ...

In griefs and pains Thy sacred Word
(Dear solace of my soul!)
Celestial comforts can afford
And all their power control

When present sufferings pain my heart
Or future terrors rise
And light and hope almost depart
From these dejected eyes

Thy powerful Word supports my hope
Sweet cordial of the mind
And bears my fainting spirit up
And bids me wait resigned

And oh whate'er of earthly bliss
Thy sovereign hand denies
Accepted at Thy throne of grace
Let this petition rise

"Give me a calm, a thankful heart
From every murmur free
The blessings of Thy grace impart
And let me live to Thee

Let the sweet hope that Thou art mine
My path of life attend
Thy presence through my journey shine
And bless its happy end"[5]

▶▶▶▶ GOING FORWARD

Have another person read this section.

Long before modern psychology, the lament psalms show that the People of God recognized the importance of naming and moving through grief rather than ignoring it. Lamenting has its place in the worship life of the community, alongside praising and celebrating. A faith that ignores or downplays times of crisis is not an honest or complete faith. Too often modern churches deal with lament only at funerals, but we do ourselves and those among us who are suffering a great disservice if we do not make a more holistic effort to deal with times of crisis together as a community. Our communal worship time needs to deal with sadness and loss; we need to provide a place where those who are suffering can find a home. The suffering are not meant to be shut out, forced to put on a happy face for the rest of us. We should be suffering with them. In the same way, when crisis strikes the community as a whole, our churches are remiss not to offer opportunities for all to grieve together, to place our pain and grief in the context of our relationship with God.[6]

But lament is not the last word. Just as the psalmist knows that God hears our prayers even when he appears to be absent, the psalmist also knows hope—that God will deliver him eventually from the suffering, in God's own time. The psalter itself shows this movement from lament to praise. The first half of the book of Psalms is weighted heavily toward psalms of lament, but the second half contains many more psalms of praise. Our journey in the with-God life will hold times of suffering and lament, even times when we feel that God is no longer with us, but if we keep calling to God, we know that our times of suffering will be temporary, and with the ultimate hope of the resurrection in mind, we will move back into praise and thanksgiving.

How does your church community make provision for those who are lamenting or suffering? How might it do better? Have you ever felt alienated from your church's worship?

REFLECTION QUESTION Again, allow each member a few moments to answer this question.

This concludes our look at lamenting. In the next chapter we will turn our attention to another avenue of prayer and worship—trusting.

⤳ After everyone has had a chance to respond, the leader reads this paragraph.

⤳ **Allow some time for members to encourage one another to read the Devotional and Scripture Readings and do the exercise in the following chapter before the next meeting.** Then invite the members to be silent for a few moments before leading them in reading the Closing Prayer aloud together.

CLOSING PRAYER

Incline your ear, O Lord, and answer me,
    for I am poor and needy,
Preserve my life, for I am devoted to you;
    save your servant who trusts in you.
You are my God; be gracious to me, O Lord,
    for to you do I cry all day long.
Gladden the soul of your servant,
    for to you, O Lord, I lift up my soul.

At the end of the Closing Prayer, the leader asks for a volunteer to lead the next meeting.

For you, O Lord, are good and forgiving,
    abounding in steadfast love to all who call on you.
Give ear, O LORD, to my prayer;
    listen to my cry of supplication.
In the day of my trouble I call on you,
    for you will answer me.

For you are great and do wondrous things;
    you alone are God.
Teach me your way, O LORD,
    that I may walk in your truth. (PS 86:1–7, 10–11a)

TAKING IT FURTHER

ADDITIONAL EXERCISE

Read Psalm 22 every day for a week, putting yourself in the place of the psalmist. Think about how God has delivered you from times of suffering and lament in the past, just like he delivered the psalmist. Trace the psalmist's movement from lament to praise and thanksgiving.

ADDITIONAL RESOURCES

Bellinger, W. H., Jr. *Psalms: Reading and Studying the Book of Praises.* Peabody, MA: Hendrickson, 1990.
Wolterstorff, Nicholas. *Lament for a Son.* Grand Rapids, MI: Eerdmans, 1987.

ADDITIONAL REFLECTION QUESTIONS

In what ways does our culture allow for or support lamenting? In times of grief in your life, would you have preferred to have had a more established custom of mourning, for example, a day-long wake or the wearing of a type of clothing that would let everyone know you were mourning?

Is there any kind of established community lament in our culture? Can you think of a time when your whole country or community was in mourning? If so, how did your church handle it?

Wolterstorff wrote about how grief isolates even those grieving from each other because each of us grieves differently. Have you experienced this in your life? Has grief brought you and your loved ones closer together or farther apart?

9 TRUSTING

DEVOTIONAL READING

PAUL GERHARDT, "Christian Trust"

> Give to the winds thy fears;
>   Hope and be undismayed;
> God hears thy sighs and counts thy tears;
>   God shall lift up thy head.
> Through waves, through clouds and storms,
>   He gently clears thy way;
> Wait thou His time; so shall the night
>   Soon end in joyous day.
>
> He everywhere hath way,
>   And all things serve His might;
> His every act pure blessing is,
>   His paths, unsullied light.
> When He makes bare His arm,
>   What shall His work withstand?
> When He His people's cause defends,
>   Who, who shall stay His hand?
>
> Leave to His sovereign sway
>   To choose and to command;
> With wonder filled, thou then shalt own
>   How wise, how strong, His hand.
> Thou comprehend'st Him not
>   Yet earth and heaven tell,
> God sits as sovereign on the throne—
>   He ruleth all things well.

✍ It is helpful for everyone to read the Devotional and Scripture Readings and do the My Life with God Exercise before the meeting. Begin the meeting with silent prayer, then move directly to Reflecting on My Life With God below.

Thou seest our weakness, Lord!
    Our hearts are known to Thee;
O lift Thou up the sinking head
    Confirm the feeble knee!
Let us, in life and death,
    Boldly Thy truth declare,
And publish with our latest breath
    Thy love and guardian care.[1]

MY LIFE WITH GOD EXERCISE

What is trust? In a dictionary it is defined as a firm belief in the reliability, truth, ability, or strength of someone or something. We sing numerous hymns and songs that encourage it—"Only Trust Him," "Trust and Obey," "Pass Me Not, O Gentle Savior," and "You Are My Hiding Place," to name only a few. Many of us have said or thought, "I'm trusting the Lord," when we have come up against a problem such as finding a job, disciplining a child, facing surgery, confronting a spouse, grieving for a loss, facing financial shortfalls, and more. But what does trusting God really mean?

For a few days we ask you to think about and meditate on the following questions: What is trust? How has trust in God been expressed in my life? What increases my trust in God? There is no need to write anything down unless you believe it will help you answer these questions. As you are pondering them, you might want to ask someone close to you what their answers would be. Once you have exhausted your reflection, read and meditate on these Bible verses for about fifteen minutes each, making sure first to ask the Holy Spirit to guide your heart and thoughts.

- Proverbs 3:5–6—"Trust in the LORD with all your heart, / and do not rely on your own insight."
- Isaiah 12:2—"Surely God is my salvation; / I will trust, and not be afraid, / for the LORD GOD is my strength and my might; / he has become my salvation."
- Philippians 2:23–24—"I hope therefore to send [Timothy] as soon as I see how things go with me; and I trust in the Lord that I will also come soon."
- 1 Peter 1:21—"Through [Jesus Christ] you have come to trust in God, who raised him from the dead and gave him glory, so that your faith and hope are set on God."

What did you learn about trust as you were meditating on the questions and the Scripture verses? Who or what do you trust?

REFLECTING ON MY LIFE WITH GOD
Allow each member a few moments to answer this question.

➤ SCRIPTURE READING: PSALM 23

✍ After everyone has had a chance to respond to the question, ask a member to read this passage from Scripture.

The LORD is my shepherd, I shall not want.
    He makes me lie down in green pastures;
he leads me beside still waters;
    he restores my soul.
He leads me in right paths
    for his name's sake.

Even though I walk through the darkest valley,
    I fear no evil;
for you are with me;
    your rod and your staff—
    they comfort me.

You prepare a table before me
    in the presence of my enemies;
you anoint my head with oil;
    my cup overflows.
Surely goodness and mercy shall follow me
    all the days of my life,
and I shall dwell in the house of the LORD
    my whole life long.

What does the image of God as your shepherd mean to you?

REFLECTION QUESTION
Allow each person a few moments to respond to this question.

➤➤ GETTING THE PICTURE

Psalm 23 contains perhaps the best-known lines in the entire Bible. The trouble with verses that are so familiar is that we often skim right over the words and their underlying meanings. For many of us the image of God as a shepherd is so far removed from our experience that it can be

✍ After a brief discussion, choose one person to read this section.

difficult to fully understand. For David, however, to whom Psalm 23 is attributed, nothing was more natural than equating God with a shepherd. When God searched among Jesse's sons for a king to replace Saul, David, the youngest, was not present because he was out tending the sheep as usual (1 Sam 16:11). That the youngest son was assigned to the job clues us in that shepherding was not an exalted position; according to Eugene Peterson, it was equivalent to babysitting for a neighbor or stocking groceries at the supermarket.[2] Yet, as David knew from experience, to the sheep their keeper was everything. He led them to water and to green pastures where they could eat; he kept them safe from predators, even sleeping with them at night. David described to Saul just how diligently he defended his sheep: "Your servant [David] used to keep sheep for his father; and whenever a lion or a bear came, and took a lamb from the flock, I went after it and struck it down, rescuing the lamb from its mouth" (1 Sam 17:34–35a). Sheep knew well the voice of their shepherd and followed him without question, trusting that he would keep them safe. It is no wonder that David and later Jesus found the shepherd such a compelling image.

In the second half of the psalm, God is portrayed as a host who prepares a table. Then the psalmist tells us that he anoints the guest's head with oil in the presence of his enemies, another illustration from David's own life. The day when the Lord and Samuel came to Jesse's house, the Lord rejected Jesse's older sons in favor of David, the lowly youngest son, the shepherd. Then he directed Samuel to anoint David's head with oil in the presence of his brothers, who must have been jealous and unbelieving (16:12–13). It can be difficult for us to understand the importance placed on birth order in biblical times, especially since God so often defied this human convention by choosing to bless younger brothers—Jacob, Joseph, now David. Deuteronomy 21:17, however, tells us that the firstborn was to receive a double portion of all that the father had. Great respect would have been accorded in the household to David's brother Eliab, Jesse's eldest son, and he would have been expected to inherit Jesse's authority upon his death. By law the eldest sons of kings were the successors to the throne (2 Chron 21:3). So for the youngest of Jesse's sons to be singled out in such a remarkable way would probably have greatly angered his brothers. David likely would have felt uncomfortable and perhaps a little frightened. He certainly would have been unprepared for such an honor; he had to trust that God knew what he was doing.

The psalm teaches us that to trust God we must begin by being obedient to him. The first step in obedience is recognizing God's voice, just as sheep know the voice of their shepherd. Jesus said, "I am the good shepherd. I know my own and my own know me, just as the Father knows me and I know the Father. And I lay down my life for the sheep. I have other sheep that do not belong to this fold. I must bring them also, and they will listen to my voice" (John 10:14–16). We must learn to distinguish the voice of God from all the other voices competing for our attention and allegiance. Second, we must commit without question to the direction in which God leads us, even if our own desires tempt us to go elsewhere. God's path can also be surprising and unexpected. We can imagine that the young shepherd David did not feel prepared to accept anointing as king, but he trusted in God's plan. Trusting is recognizing that God knows better for us than we know for ourselves, that the path on which he leads us will lead us to nourishment, that he sees more than we can see.

Have another member read this section.

This trust in the Lord is not a passive mind-set but an active one. We *choose* to follow him. We choose to listen to his voice. We also choose to let him carry out justice in his own way. We do not have to be afraid of places and people that threaten us; at the same time it is not up to us to defend ourselves. Just as David described how he would strike down anything that harmed a member of his flock, trusting the Lord is also expecting *his* justice. Committing our way to the Lord means giving to him all of our feelings of fear, resentment, anger, and jealousy.[3] When we trust God in all of life's circumstances, bringing justice to our situation is God's responsibility, not ours. Sometimes in the short term we may not agree with God's solution, but in the long term it will be best for us and all concerned. When we trust God for our situation, we will be free to fight for justice in the lives of others. We can expend our energies on behalf of others rather than in looking out for ourselves.

To trust in the Lord brings the abundant life Jesus promised: "I came that they may have life, and have it abundantly" (John 10:10). "My cup overflows," wrote the psalmist. "Surely goodness and mercy shall follow me all the days of my life (vv 5b–6a)." God's love is not begrudging or scarce but pursues us and overwhelms us with its abundance. If we trust in him, this overflowing love will be our reward.

Finally, for those of us on this side of Jesus's resurrection, the trust described in the Old Testament enlarges to become what is termed in the New Testament as faith. Interestingly, in the NRSV there are seventy references to trust in the Old Testament and only four references in the New Testament, a 17.5 to 1 ratio. For faith, the opposite is true: there is a 1 to 13.33 ratio. Even though the dictionary lists *faith* as a synonym for *trust,* there is a difference. The psalmist and other writers of the Old Testament, even the statements attributed to God, tied trust to blessings in the present life. Very seldom was anything mentioned about life beyond the grave (see Psalm 22:29 and Job 19:25–27). But the resurrection of Jesus three days after his death changed all that. Now faith in Jesus Christ calls us to believe he will provide not only for us here and now but for our existence into eternity. In addition, faith in Jesus Christ calls us to live in the spirit of the Old Testament saints—"to do justice, and to love kindness, and to walk humbly with your God" (Micah 6:8b). As Jesus's disciples in the kingdom that is here and now but not yet fully realized, we place everything we are—physical, mental, emotional, spiritual—on the altar as a "living sacrifice" (Rom 12:1). We serve Jesus not because we are physically born into his family, as were the Israelites, but because we are spiritually grafted into his family. It is a privilege to love and serve him.

REFLECTION QUESTION
Allow each person a few moments to respond.

How is trust a part of your faith?

▶▶▶▶ POINTING TO GOD

✍ Choose one member to read this section.

The names of legendary Christian music couple Bill and Gloria Gaither have become synonymous with Christian music. From their beginnings in Southern gospel to today's *The Gaither Music Hour* to the extraordinarily successful Homecoming concert series, the Gaithers and their music have become known as a bridge between Southern gospel and contemporary Christian music. The two have written more than six hundred songs, usually with Bill composing the music and Gloria the lyrics, and have received numerous honors, including Doves and Grammys. Bill was named the Christian "Songwriter of the Century" by the American Society of Composers and Publishers in 2000.

But it took a great deal of trust in God to get where they are today. After graduating from music school and putting all his energy into a

PRAYER AND WORSHIP

gospel quartet that ended as a dismal failure, nineteen-year-old Bill came to the heartbreaking conclusion that he didn't have what it took to be a gospel singer. "For the first time in my life, I truly placed my life in God's hands," he explains.[4] He moved back in with his parents and enrolled in college but kept singing on the weekends. He formed a trio with family members, but that soon fell apart as well. While working as an English teacher at a local high school, he decided to turn his hand to writing gospel songs and finally experienced some modest success. Things really started to take shape when he met and married Gloria Sickal, who soon became his writing partner. As their popularity grew, trusting in God to show them the next steps remained a constant theme in their lives as well as in their music, as described in "Gentle Shepherd," their beautiful hymn about trusting in Jesus as the shepherd who leads us:

> Gentle Shepherd, come and lead us,
> For we need You to help us find our way.
> Gentle Shepherd, come and feed us,
> For we need Your strength from day to day.
> There's no other we can turn to
> Who can help us face another day;
> Gentle Shepherd, come and lead us,
> For we need You to help us find our way.[5]

▶▶▶▶▶ GOING FORWARD

It is clear that trust is a central part of the Christian life. Without trust in God, we cannot have faith. Trust is a choice to give God control of our lives, to believe that he will provide for our physical needs. Not our wants, but our *needs*. It is sometimes difficult to turn over the reins, but when we release control to God, we receive a wonderful freedom in knowing that he is in charge and knows what is best for us.

Trusting God is also feeling settled in matters of our future life. Death becomes for us a matter of going from one room to another, not a rupturing or extinguishing of who we are as individuals. When born into this world we are eternal; we have to make a decision where we want to spend eternity—with God or apart from God. We trust in God that our eternity will be with him.

✍ Have another person read this section.

How can we demonstrate trusting God in our lives?

⚑ After everyone has had a chance to respond, the leader reads this paragraph.

⚑ **Allow some time for members to encourage one another to read the Devotional and Scripture Readings and do the exercise in the following chapter before the next meeting.** Then invite the members to be silent for a few moments before leading them in reading the Closing Prayer aloud together.

⚑ At the end of the Closing Prayer, the leader asks for a volunteer to lead the next meeting.

This concludes our look at trusting. In the next chapter we will turn our attention to another avenue of prayer and worship—praising.

CLOSING PRAYER

Incline your ear, O LORD, and answer me,
> for I am poor and needy,
Preserve my life, for I am devoted to you;
> save your servant who trusts in you.
You are my God; be gracious to me, O Lord,
> for to you do I cry all day long.
Gladden the soul of your servant,
> for to you, O Lord, I lift up my soul.
For you, O Lord, are good and forgiving,
> abounding in steadfast love to all who call on you.
Give ear, O LORD, to my prayer;
> listen to my cry of supplication.
In the day of my trouble I call on you,
> for you will answer me.

For you are great and do wondrous things;
> you alone are God.
Teach me your way, O LORD,
> that I may walk in your truth. (PS 86:1–7, 10–11a)

TAKING IT FURTHER

Trusting in God has a marked effect on those around us. When it is obvious that God is in charge of our life, it is an incredible witness and example to everyone we encounter. Think about who in your life has influenced you with their extraordinary trust in God. Consider letting them know about the impact they have had on you, if you have not already done so. Ask them what practices help them maintain such trust. Next, seek to be aware of the impact your trust in God (or lack thereof) might be having on those around you.

Gaither Vocal Band. *Best of the Gaither Vocal Band.* EMI CMG, 2004.

Gerhardt, Paul. "Christian Trust." In *Religious Poems*, translated by John Wesley. New York: Thomas Y. Crowell, n.d.

Powell, Mark Allen. "There's Just Something About That Man." *Christianity Today* (2004), available at http://www.christianitytoday.com/ct/2004/004/1.32.html.

ADDITIONAL RESOURCES

How is trusting linked to waiting?

ADDITIONAL REFLECTION QUESTIONS

What are some times in your life when you failed to trust in God and perhaps acted rashly? What were the results?

What is the opposite of trusting God?

10 PRAISING

KEY SCRIPTURE: Psalm 150

DEVOTIONAL READING

THOMAS MERTON, *Praying the Psalms*

To praise God!

Do we know what it means to praise? To adore? To give glory?

Praise is cheap today. Everything is praised. Soap, beer, toothpaste, clothing, mouthwash, movie stars, all the latest gadgets which are supposed to make life more comfortable—everything is constantly being "praised." Praise is now so overdone that everybody is sick of it, and since everything is "praised" with the official hollow enthusiasm of the radio announcer, it turns out in the end that *nothing* is praised. Praise has become empty. Nobody really wants to use it.

Are there any superlatives left for God? They have all been wasted on foods and quack medicines. There is no word left to express our adoration of Him who alone is Holy, who alone is Lord.

So we go to Him to ask help and to get out of being punished, and to mumble that we need a better job, more money, more of the things that are praised by the advertisements. And we wonder why our prayer is so often dead—gaining its only life, borrowing its only urgency from the fact that we need these things so badly.

But we do not really think we need God. Least of all do we think we need to praise Him.

It is quite possible that our lack of interest in the Psalms conceals a secret lack of interest in God. For if we have no real interest in praising Him, it shows that we have never realized who He is. For when one becomes conscious of who God really is, and when one realizes that He who is Almighty, and infinitely Holy, has "done great things to us," the only possible reaction is the cry of half-articulated exultation that bursts from the depths of our being in amazement at the tremendous, inexplicable goodness of God to men....

> It is helpful for everyone to read the Devotional and Scripture Readings and do the My Life with God Exercise before the meeting. Begin the meeting with silent prayer, then move directly to Reflecting on My Life With God below.

When we praise God, says St. Augustine, there must be order in our praise. It must be intelligent, spiritual. We must not be carried away by emotionalism. Nor should we on the other hand be so "objective" that there is no longer anything personal in our prayer to God. In order that we may remain on the straight road, turning neither to the right nor to the left, "the best way is to seek the way of praise in the Scriptures of God." (*Melius iter laudis in Scriptura Dei quaerimus.*)

St. Augustine adds that God has taught us to praise Him, in the Psalms, not in order that He may get something out of this praise, but in order *that we may be made better by it.* Praising God in the words of the Psalms, we can come to know Him better. Knowing Him better we love Him better, loving Him better we find our happiness in Him. "Therefore, because He knew that this would be for our benefit, He made himself more loveable to us by praising Himself." These words, taken from St. Augustine's commentary on Psalm 144, are supplemented by others in his *De Doctrina Christiana,* where he says: "God wants to be loved not in order that He may get something out of it, but in order that those who love Him may receive an eternal reward. And this reward is God Himself, whom they love." (*De Doct. Christ.* i:29.)[1]

MY LIFE WITH GOD EXERCISE

Thomas Merton describes how praise of God has been cheapened and emptied of meaning by the overuse of praise in describing consumer goods, celebrities, and gadgets. This trend has led to a scarcity of words to describe God, an understanding of prayer as a way to get what we want, and an attitude that we don't need God, which is reflected in a decreased interest in the Psalms, where we learn who he is and how to praise him. C. S. Lewis expressed a similar sentiment in *Reflections on the Psalms,* as he examined his feelings toward praising God. Initially, as he wrote, when he started "to draw near to belief in God," the idea of praising God was a "stumbling block." Even more difficult was "the suggestion that God Himself demanded it."[2]

As Lewis thought more about his feelings and examined the world around him, he wrote:

But the most obvious fact about praise—whether of God or anything—strangely escaped me. I thought of it in terms of compliment, approval, or the giving of honour. I had never noticed that all

PRAYER AND WORSHIP

enjoyment spontaneously overflows into praise unless (sometimes even if) shyness or the fear of boring others is deliberately brought in to check it. The world rings with praise—lovers praising their mistresses, readers their favourite poet, walkers praising the countryside, players praising their favourite game—praise of weather, wines, dishes, actors, motors, horses, colleges, countries, historical personages, children, flowers, mountains, rare stamps, rare beetles, even sometimes politicians or scholars. . . . I think we delight to praise what we enjoy because the praise not merely expresses but completes the enjoyment; it is its appointed consummation.[3]

Are Merton and Lewis right? Do we find it difficult to praise God? If we do, why? Do we lack an interest in God because we don't realize who he is? Or do we really not enjoy God? Or are there other reasons? As a way to discover your genuine feelings toward giving praise to God, set aside fifteen minutes each day for about six days to sit before him, and ponder and answer the following questions of examen (a daily prayer method of discernment). We suggest limiting yourself to one question per day.

What is my attitude toward praising God?

How has my background affected that attitude?

How are my vocation or present life circumstances affecting that attitude?

How is the culture affecting that attitude?

Does anything need to be changed about my attitude? If so, what?

What can I do to change, refocus, or nurture my attitude?

Feel free to write down the answers to these questions here, on the last page of this chapter, or perhaps in your journal. If you don't write them down, be sure to make a mental note of them so that you remember to do those things you suggest in the answer to the last question. It will also help to revisit your answers in several months to check on the progress you are making in your relationship with God and praise of him.

REFLECTING ON MY LIFE WITH GOD
Allow each member a few moments to answer this question.

What did you find out about your attitude toward praising God? What circumstances in your life contributed to that attitude?

▶ SCRIPTURE READING: PSALM 150

☙ After everyone has had a chance to respond to the question, ask a member to read this passage from Scripture.

Praise the LORD!
Praise God in his sanctuary;
    praise him in his mighty firmament!
Praise him for his mighty deeds;
    praise him according to his surpassing greatness!

Praise him with trumpet sound;
    praise him with lute and harp!
Praise him with tambourine and dance;
    praise him with strings and pipe!
Praise him with clanging cymbals;
    praise him with loud clashing cymbals!
Let everything that breathes praise the LORD!
Praise the LORD!

REFLECTION QUESTION
Allow each person a few moments to respond to this question.

Name one thing that particularly stands out to you about Psalm 150.

▶▶ GETTING THE PICTURE

☙ After a brief discussion, choose one person to read this section.

Though very short, Psalm 150 manages to work the word *praise* into every line. These brief verses are packed with who, where, why, and how we should praise, giving us a peek into the worship practices of the Israelites. Psalm 150 is the last in a series of psalms in book 5 (107–50), through which are woven themes of prayer and praise. Psalms 113–18, 120–36, and 146–50 are considered Hallel, or praise, psalms. Psalm 150 was used in the Israelites' worship of God, but exactly how has been lost over the centuries.

When we first read Psalm 150, we notice the breadth of themes in the first two verses. Praise for God encompasses earth and heaven, what God does, and who he is. We find the same themes in the Christian doxology. "Praise God, from whom all blessings flow" cites what God does; "Praise him, all creatures here below" deals with earth; "Praise him, above ye heav'nly host" covers heaven; and "Praise Father, Son, and Holy Ghost" addresses who God is.[4] It is no wonder that scholars consider Psalm 150 to be the doxology to the psalter. But Psalm 150 is more comprehensive and expressive than the Christian doxology. In addition to including earth and heaven in the praise of God, the psalmist commands that all instruments be used to praise God and that everything which breathes air praise God.

Some of the instruments named appear very early in the biblical record, suggesting that the Israelites used Psalm 150 in the Solomonic Temple. For example, horns and trumpets are mentioned in Numbers 10:1–10 to call a convocation, and in 1 Kings 1:34, 39, and 41–43 to announce the ascension of Solomon to the throne of his father, David. Of course, stringed instruments—harps and lyres—appear many times. David played a lyre to soothe King Saul when an evil spirit tormented him (1 Sam 16:23). A harp appears once in 1 Samuel (10:5) and numerous times in the Psalms (see 33:2, 43:4, 49:4, 71:22, 81:2, 92:3, and 144:9). In Exodus 15:20, Miriam, Moses's sister, plays a tambourine as the children of Israel celebrate their escape from Egypt and God's victory over the Egyptian army at their crossing of the sea. The pipe or flute was also used at celebrations (1 Kings 1:40; Isa 5:12). The biggest puzzle is the difference between "clanging cymbals" and "loud crashing cymbals," other than their sound. Clanging cymbals could be like the little metal finger cymbals belly dancers play while performing; these are similar to ancient Egyptian castanets like those represented on the tomb of a sacred musician from the second century BC. They might also be like the cymbals used by the Chinese in their celebrations, whereas loud crashing cymbals could resemble the ones found in Egyptian images and currently used in marching bands and symphonies.[5] In any event, Hebrew worship would have included musicians singing psalms and playing instruments, just as many Christians continue to do in worship today.

▶▶▶ GOING DEEPER

Since at present we are earthbound, our eternal life of praise to God "must begin here on earth."[6] According to the psalmist, this earthbound praise was to take place in the sanctuary, God's dwelling place on earth (Lev 26:11; Pss 63:2, 68:35). From his perspective, the sanctuary was the tabernacle built by the Hebrews as they were wandering in the desert, and the Temple built by Solomon (Exod 40:34–38; 1 Kings 8:10–13).

✐ Have another member read this section.

Later, praise of God centered around the synagogues and the second Temple. Now, for Christians at least, with an understanding that we are each temples of the Holy Spirit, we know that we can praise God wherever we are—at church, in our homes, as we travel, when we work (1 Cor 3:16–17; 2 Cor 6:16). Though earthbound, our praise is not confined to one place or a set time. Along with the heavenly hosts, we are to praise at all times and in all places.

How can we enumerate the many things God has done for which we are called to praise him? One of the marvelous features of ancient and contemporary Judaism is its many festivals where congregants recall the mighty works of God. This historical memory is integral to the celebration of Passover, Yom Kippur, and Hanukkah. It is vividly expressed in the Song of Moses (Exod 15:1–18) and permeates psalms too numerous to list. In the Church, giving praise to God by recalling what he has done for us as the People of God is woven into the calendar in the form of holy days—Easter, Pentecost, Christmas—and the liturgy. These special times of praise give us a chance to supplement the individual praise we give to God during our private times with him, and are important for the growth of our own relationship with God and with those in our community of faith.

A component of praising God is coming to understand who he is, as best we can. There are several activities that help—study, prayer, meditation, discussion, and praise. When we spend time meditating on and praising God for all the wonderful things he has done, it helps us understand more about God—what God values, how he acts in history, how much he loves us. As long as we live, however, we will never be able to grasp all of God's love, steadfastness, concern, might, and as the psalmist wrote, greatness. The totality of God's greatness is a mystery and will remain a mystery to us while we are bound to this physical earth. At some time and in some way, we who "see in a mirror, dimly, . . . will see face to face." We who "know only in part; . . . will know fully" (1 Cor 13:12). It is a mystery. All we can do is accept the mystery and praise God.

The psalm also teaches that we should welcome any instrument that helps us praise God. The Israelites did not hesitate to use horns and timbrels (tambourines) and strings and wind instruments and cymbals as they praised God. The message of Psalm 150 seems to be that God could care less what instruments we use or when we play a wrong note or sing off key when we are praising him. What seems important is that we obey the palmist's last command—"Let everything that breathes praise the LORD!"—and take to heart Augustine's counsel, "The Christian should be an alleluia from head to foot."

What aspects of praise do you or your church do well? Praising God in all times and places? Praising God for all of his wonderful acts throughout history and in your life and the life of those around you? Praising God with any instrument at hand? What do you feel might be missing?

REFLECTION QUESTION
Allow each person a few moments to respond.

▶▶▶▶ POINTING TO GOD

A classic worship piece that comes to mind when thinking of praise is George Frideric Handel's "Hallelujah Chorus" from the *Messiah*. Handel, a German by birth who later became a British citizen, is considered one of the most notable composers of the prolific Baroque period, but at the time he composed *Messiah,* his best-known work, his popularity was at a low point. Even though he had suffered a stroke that partially paralyzed his left side, he wrote the music for *Messiah* in just twenty-one days.[7] Handel is said to have described composing the piece as a religious experience, saying "I did think I did see all Heaven before me and the great God Himself."[8] Although it is often performed at Christmastime, Handel originally envisioned it as a piece for Lent and Easter. Upon being congratulated by a nobleman on its enthusiastic reception in London (King George II rose to his feet during the "Hallelujah Chorus"), Handel said, "My Lord, I should be sorry if I only entertained them; I wished to make them better."[9]

✄ Choose one member to read this section.

Handel's lofty goals aside, *Messiah* was unlike any other oratorio of its time. According to music historian R. A. Streatfield, *Messiah* was "the first instance in the history of music of an attempt to view the mighty drama of human redemption from an artistic viewpoint."[10] Although Handel composed the music for *Messiah,* literary scholar Charles Jennens prepared the libretto for the music from verses carefully selected from the Old and New Testaments, encompassing the creation, Jesus's suffering, death, and resurrection, and the redemption of humankind. The words from these verses sung in Handel's mighty choruses and stirring vocal solos were and are an undeniably stirring combination. It is hard to imagine, since it is fairly universally loved today, but not everyone appreciated *Messiah* when it debuted in Dublin in 1742 and then in London. The theater was considered to be vulgar and profane, not a place for music of a religious nature. And Handel himself, although he had previously written operas based on biblical stories, was known as a secular composer. Dean Jonathan Swift, the author of *Gulliver's Travels,* threatened to prevent the St. Patrick's Cathedral singers from participating in the Dublin opening of *Messiah,* but eventually relented. For the London premiere, Handel advertised his work as "A Sacred Oratorio" in order to avoid any charges of blasphemy.[11]

Here are the Scriptures Jennens chose for the "Hallelujah Chorus" at the end of Act 2:

> Hallelujah! for the Lord God Omnipotent reigneth [Rev 19:6].
>
> The kingdom of this world is become the kingdom of our Lord, and of His Christ; and He shall reign for ever and ever [Rev 11:15].
>
> King of Kings, and Lord of Lords [Rev 19:16].
>
> Hallelujah![12]

The "Hallelujah!" repeated so often in the chorus is based on the Hebrew word *hllwyh* (praise be to Yah), which is translated "alleluia" in Latin and "hallelujah" in English. Interestingly, this very Hebrew word, *hllwyh,* is also translated as "praise" so many times in Psalm 150, our Scripture Reading. Like Psalm 150, Handel's work calls for praising God with many instruments.

▸▸▸▸▸▸ GOING FORWARD

Have another person read this section.

None of us is exempt from praising, even if we have a poor singing voice or no ability to play an instrument. We can all enjoy music even if we feel it is not one of our spiritual gifts; after all, God hears our praise even when it is sung off key! But there are other ways to praise God: by reciting his great and mighty acts, by thanking him constantly for all he is and all he does. As we read in the Devotional Reading, God asks us to praise him not because he gets something out of it but rather "in order that we may be made better by it." This is also why Augustine urges us to praise with order and intelligence—because it is in praising God that we better know him and better understand who he is. We should praise him with our whole bodies and whole hearts, using whatever musical instruments we like, yet we should also be aware that our minds need to be involved in praising, as we constantly seek to understand more of God's nature.

But there is even more to praising God. As C. S. Lewis says, praise is the consummation of enjoyment. Speaking about how much we enjoy, appreciate, and admire something helps us to enjoy it all the more. The very act of praising deepens our appreciation and love for God, which in turn begets more praising—a happy, God-ordained cycle.

In your life, how has praising God helped you to understand and love God more?

REFLECTION QUESTION
Again, allow each member a few moments to answer this question.

This concludes our look at praising. In the next chapter we will turn our attention to another avenue of prayer and worship—thanking.

⤢ After everyone has had a chance to respond, the leader reads this paragraph.

⤢ **Allow some time for members to encourage one another to read the Devotional and Scripture Readings and do the exercise in the following chapter before the next meeting.** Then invite the members to be silent for a few moments before leading them in reading the Closing Prayer aloud together.

⤢ At the end of the Closing Prayer, the leader asks for a volunteer to lead the next meeting.

CLOSING PRAYER

Incline your ear, O Lord, and answer me,
 for I am poor and needy,
Preserve my life, for I am devoted to you;
 save your servant who trusts in you.
You are my God; be gracious to me, O Lord,
 for to you do I cry all day long.
Gladden the soul of your servant,
 for to you, O Lord, I lift up my soul.
For you, O Lord, are good and forgiving,
 abounding in steadfast love to all who call on you.
Give ear, O Lord, to my prayer;
 listen to my cry of supplication.
In the day of my trouble I call on you,
 for you will answer me.

For you are great and do wondrous things;
 you alone are God.
Teach me your way, O Lord,
 that I may walk in your truth. (PS 86:1–7, 10–11a)

TAKING IT FURTHER

ADDITIONAL EXERCISE

In the Devotional Reading, Thomas Merton quotes Augustine's admonition to praise God "with order." Our praise should be intelligent and spiritual, according to Augustine, but we should be careful not to be "carried away by emotionalism." What do you think Augustine means by praising with order? When you praise God, do you do it with order and intelligence? Conversely, are you at times carried away by emotionalism? Why do you think Augustine sees that as a danger? This week, as you praise God, in daily prayer or in your small group or worship service, focus on praising God with order.

Praising

ADDITIONAL RESOURCES

Lewis, C. S. *Reflections on the Psalms*. New York: Harvest/Harcourt Brace Jovanovich, 1958.

Merton, Thomas. *Praying the Psalms*. Collegeville, MN: Liturgical, 1956.

ADDITIONAL REFLECTION QUESTIONS

Have you ever heard Handel's Messiah? If so, what was your reaction to it?

What piece of music or style of music is the embodiment of praise to you? Why?

How do you feel most comfortable praising God? Alone or with others? With music and singing or with prayer and meditation? Why? Consider challenging yourself to praise God in ways that are less familiar.

11 THANKING

DEVOTIONAL READING

EDWARD M. BOUNDS, *The Essentials of Prayer*

Prayer, praise and thanksgiving all go in company. A close relationship exists between them. Praise and thanksgiving are so near alike that it is not easy to distinguish between them or define them separately. The Scriptures join these three things together. Many are the causes for thanksgiving and praise. The Psalms are filled with many songs of praise and hymns of thanksgiving, all pointing back to the results of prayer. Thanksgiving includes gratitude. In fact thanksgiving is but the expression of an inward conscious gratitude to God for mercies received. Gratitude is an inward emotion of the soul, involuntarily arising therein, while thanksgiving is the voluntary expression of gratitude.

Thanksgiving is oral, positive, active. It is the giving out of something to God. Thanksgiving comes out into the open. Gratitude is secret, silent, negative, passive, not showing its being till expressed in praise and thanksgiving. Gratitude is felt in the heart. Thanksgiving is the expression of that inward feeling.

Thanksgiving is just what the word itself signifies—the giving of thanks to God. It is giving something to God in words which we feel at heart for blessings received. Gratitude arises from a contemplation of the goodness of God. It is bred by serious meditation on what God has done for us. Both gratitude and thanksgiving point to, and have to do with God and His mercies. The heart is consciously grateful to God. The soul gives expression to that heartfelt gratitude to God in words or acts.

Gratitude is born of meditation on God's grace and mercy. "The Lord hath done great things for us, whereof we are glad." Herein we see the value of serious meditation. "My meditation of him shall be sweet."

It is helpful for everyone to read the Devotional and Scripture Readings and do the My Life with God Exercise before the meeting. Begin the meeting with silent prayer, then move directly to Reflecting on My Life With God below.

Praise is begotten by gratitude and a conscious obligation to God for mercies given. As we think of mercies past, the heart is inwardly moved to gratitude.

> "I love to think on mercies past,
> And future good implore;
> And all my cares and sorrows cast
> On Him whom I adore."

Love is the child of gratitude. Love grows as gratitude is felt, and then breaks out into praise and thanksgiving to God: "I love the Lord because he hath heard my voice and my supplication." Answered prayers cause gratitude, and gratitude brings forth a love that declares it will not cease praying: "Because he hath inclined his ear unto me, therefore will I call upon him as long as I live." Gratitude and love move to larger and increased praying.

Paul appeals to the Romans to dedicate themselves wholly to God, a living sacrifice, and the constraining motive is the mercies of God:

> "I beseech you, therefore, brethren, by the mercies of God, that ye present your bodies a living sacrifice, holy, acceptable unto God, which is your reasonable service."

Consideration of God's mercies not only begets gratitude, but induces a large consecration to God of all we have and are. So that prayer, thanksgiving and consecration are all linked together inseparably.

Gratitude and thanksgiving always looks back at the past though it may also take in the present. But prayer always looks to the future. Thanksgiving deals with things already received. Prayer deals with things desired, asked for and expected. Prayer turns to gratitude and praise when the things asked for have been granted by God.[1]

MY LIFE WITH GOD EXERCISE

Edward M. Bounds makes the statement, "Praise and thanksgiving are so near alike that it is not easy to distinguish between them or define them separately." In this excerpt from *The Essentials of Prayer*, he discusses the source of thanksgiving—gratitude—and what it is: "the giving of thanks to God."

Although thanksgiving and praise are closely related, it is helpful to distinguish between the two, because in reflecting on Bounds's thoughts, we discover that we can praise God in song and hymn for who he is and what he has done without thanking him. Praise centers on adoration of God, while thanksgiving focuses on giving thanks to God. Praise focuses on who God is, thanksgiving on what he is doing and has done for us. Praise of God often leads to thanksgiving.

Both the Hebrew and Greek languages distinguish between praise and thanksgiving. In fact, Hebrew has a dozen words that are translated as "praise" in English, only two of which can be translated as either "praise" or "thanksgiving." In Greek, seven words can be translated by "praise," but only one Greek word and its derivatives are always translated as "be thankful," "thanksgiving," "thanks," and so on. That word is *eucharistio,* the source of the English word *Eucharist.*

With this in mind, we would like you to read Bounds's essay about thanksgiving several times, maybe twice a day, to savor its richness. Try to read it slowly, chewing on the words and absorbing them into your heart. Once you feel you have digested as much as you can, reflect on what you have to thank God for. It might be helpful to make a list to keep before you as you offer your thanks in prayer. Or you might draw a picture or write a poem. Whichever option you choose, take your time with it. There is certainly no shortage of things, in each of our lives, for which to be thankful. Perhaps you can think on the first day about things in your own life to give thanks for, the next day about your immediate family, then your extended family, your friends, your church, your community, your nation, the world, and so on.

As the second part of the exercise, when you go to a service where the Eucharist, or Communion, is celebrated, be aware of partaking as an opportunity to thank God. Not only does the Eucharist give us an opportunity to remember and thank God for what he has done for us through the birth, life, death, and resurrection of Jesus Christ: it provides us a chance to thank him for what he will do in the future. As Bounds writes, "Prayer always looks to the future," and at the end of the eucharistic ritual, there is a strong emphasis upon the future: "For as often as you eat this bread and drink the cup, you proclaim the Lord's death *until he comes*" (1 Cor 11:26, emphasis added).

How did thanking God for all of the blessings in your life and in the lives of those around you make you feel? If you have had a chance to celebrate Eucharist since doing the exercise, how did it help you experience thanksgiving?

REFLECTING ON MY LIFE WITH GOD
Allow each member a few moments to answer this question.

► SCRIPTURE READING: LUKE 22:14–22

After everyone has had a chance to respond to the question, ask a member to read this passage from Scripture.

When the hour came, [Jesus] took his place at the table, and the apostles with him. He said to them, "I have eagerly desired to eat this Passover with you before I suffer; for I tell you, I will not eat it until it is fulfilled in the kingdom of God." Then he took a cup, and after giving thanks he said, "Take this and divide it among yourselves; for I tell you that from now on I will not drink of the fruit of the vine until the kingdom of God comes." Then he took a loaf of bread, and when he had given thanks, he broke it and gave it to them, saying, "This is my body, which is given for you. Do this in remembrance of me." And he did the same with the cup after supper, saying, "This cup that is poured out for you is the new covenant in my blood. But see, the one who betrays me is with me, and his hand is on the table. For the Son of Man is going as it has been determined, but woe to that one by whom he is betrayed!"

What does reading or rereading this passage add to your understanding of the Eucharist?

REFLECTION QUESTION
Allow each person a few moments to respond to this question.

►► GETTING THE PICTURE

After a brief discussion, choose one person to read this section.

To grasp the significance of the practice variously called Eucharist, the Lord's Supper, or Communion, which Jesus instituted on the night before his crucifixion, we must first understand its roots in the Jewish festival of Passover. Passover is the most important festival in Jewish life and, by conservative estimates, has been celebrated for at least three thousand years. Held in the first month of the Jewish calendar, Passover recalls the Israelites' deliverance from slavery in Egypt. In the earliest tradition (see Exodus 12), the family chose a lamb that it would slaughter at twilight. During the three days between its selection and slaughter the lamb became a household pet. After it was killed, the lamb's blood was smeared on the lintel, the support above the door. The meat was boiled and eaten with unleavened bread and bitter herbs. The lamb symbolized an innocent animal giving its life for the redemption of the family; the unleavened bread (*matzot*) symbolized the haste in which the children of Israel left Egypt, and the bitter herbs symbolized the bitterness of their slavery.

Passover is the ultimate festival of freedom and redemption for the Jewish people. The ritual altered slightly as the centuries rolled by. In Hezekiah's time, "the priests purified the people, and the Levites oversaw the slaughter of the paschal lamb."[2] During Josiah's reign, the priests were sprinkling blood on the people who came to celebrate the festival at the Temple rather than smearing it on the lintels of the Israelites' houses. By the time Jesus lived, Passover had been combined with another festival, the Festival of Unleavened Bread (Luke 22:1). Beginning the day after Passover, for seven days the Israelites cleansed their dwellings of leaven and ate *matzot*. On the first and seventh days of the festival, the family spent time together, abstaining from work.

The above Scripture gives the details of how Jesus changed the meaning of the Passover meal for his disciples. His ministry is finished. On Sunday, riding a young donkey, he had been welcomed into Jerusalem by crowds waving palm branches and shouting "Hosanna." Monday through Thursday, he taught in the Temple and confronted the religious leaders. Jesus's popularity among the crowds gathering to celebrate the Passover festival and his pointed teaching inflamed his opponents so much that the priests and Pharisees "were looking for a way to put Jesus to death, for they were afraid of the people" (Luke 22:2). In other words, they were afraid the people would try to make Jesus their religious leader; he had become a threat to their livelihoods and powerful positions. At this point, Judas approached the religious leaders and offered to betray Jesus for money. On the first day of the Festival of Unleavened Bread, Jesus's disciples asked him where he wanted to eat the Passover meal. He gave them specific instructions, and during this meal he reveals to the disciples that he will be betrayed and put to death, and institutes the Lord's Supper.

Only after Jesus's death and resurrection did the significance of the shift in the meaning of Passover for his followers become clear. In a letter from the apostle Paul to the fellowship in Corinth, we find details regarding the institution and place of the Eucharist in the worship of the Church. Paul writes at length to those who were experiencing divisions and dissension during the celebration of Eucharist. He uses the term *the Lord's Supper* for the practice (1 Cor 11:20) and emphasizes that it is an observance of fellowship when he refers to the cup as a "koinonia" (communion or sharing) of the blood of Christ and the body as the "koinonia" of the body of Christ. By writing this, Paul affirmed that those who shared together in the Lord's Supper were then bound together, made one.[3] Earlier in his letter to the Corinthians, Paul writes, "For our paschal lamb, Christ, has been sacrificed" (5:7); Peter writes, "With the precious blood of Christ, like that of a lamb without defect or blemish" (1 Peter 1:19); and "the Lamb that was slaughtered" is the central figure in John's book of Revelation (5:6, 12). All point to the fact that Jesus Christ is the human lamb whose sacrifice is for all humans.

▶▶▶ GOING DEEPER

✍ Have another member read this section.

Taking Eucharist is an important way we remember and thank Jesus Christ. Unique among all the practices of the Church, the Lord's Supper was established by the founder and foundation of the Church himself. Taking Communion makes space for us to remember what Jesus Christ did—laying down his life that we might have new life—and continues to do in our lives. No other ritual of the Church emphasizes this type of active remembrance. We may have times in our local fellowship to remember what other members have done for us or for each other and to thank them for it. But we know when we partake of the Lord's Supper we are joining uncounted numbers of Jesus's disciples who have lived before us, those who are alive today, and those who will live in the future in remembrance of what Jesus Christ has done and will do.

Participating in Eucharist reminds us that disciples of Jesus Christ are under a new covenant. Passover gives the Jewish community a wonderful opportunity to thank God for his covenant with them and for the wonderful way he redeemed them from slavery in Egypt and brought them to freedom. Similarly, the ritual of Communion reminds us that in his birth, life, death, and resurrection, Jesus Christ brought us to freedom: "For freedom Christ has set us free" (Gal 5:1). And our destiny is to spend eternity with him in "an all-inclusive community of loving persons with God himself at the very center of this community as its prime Sustainer and most glorious Inhabitant."[4]

And last, during Communion the Church gathers as a community, not as individuals. We celebrate what we have in common, not our differences. Regardless of how we came to be in the fellowship of those who follow Christ, we can meet around the Lord's Supper as fellow travelers in the with-God life. The Eucharist is the great leveler, where people of all skin colors and ethnic backgrounds and occupations and social standings are equal. It makes no difference whether we have a pristine background or numerous failures, whether we are doctors or homeless;

we all remember and thank Christ for his sacrifice. The Lord's Supper is for everyone who declares that Jesus Christ is Lord. It is the ultimate means of giving thanks for the ultimate gift, for which we are most grateful.

How does Communion lead to thanksgiving?

REFLECTION QUESTION
Allow each person a few moments to respond.

▶▶▶▶ POINTING TO GOD

✍ Choose one member to read this section.

The Eucharist as established by Jesus is the origin of not only our modern-day practice of taking Communion but also our various church services, which grew around this central practice. The manner in which the disciples continued their practice of the Eucharist and gathered for prayers led to today's liturgy, the standardized collection of hymns, prayers, and Scripture selections for each day's celebration of Mass in the Roman Catholic Church and some Protestant churches. Perhaps the church figure who has had the greatest impact on the liturgy is the sixth-century pope St. Gregory I, also known as Gregory the Great.

During his fourteen-year tenure as pope, Gregory standardized the church liturgy, with its orderly progression through thanksgiving and consecration to the high point of the sharing of the Eucharist. He is also believed to have organized, adapted, and introduced into the liturgy the plainchant style of sacred music we now know as Gregorian chant, the official liturgical music of the Catholic Church. A chant is a melody performed solely by the human voice, whether in unison or in harmony.[5] Gregorian chant used verses taken from the psalms and was meant to closely match the spoken rhythms and inflections of the text; chant is thought to be similar to the way the Israelites originally sang the psalms. This chanting can sound simple, since it is performed monophonically and without accompaniment, but in fact it is a complex musical system of eight modes, fixed intervals between notes, and free time (having no regular beat or accent). Gregory is not known to have written any chant himself, but he is credited with making it the important part of the Catholic Mass that it remains today. Chanting is done by the celebrant and his assistants during various parts of the Mass, such as the Introit, the Kyrie, and the Offertory, gradually building up to the high point of the liturgy, the Eucharist. In so reforming the Mass,

Gregory added significantly to the ways the Church through her history has thanked God through Holy Communion.

Gregorian chant is still considered the "supreme model for sacred music."[6] It is truly liturgical music, which scholar Stephen Thuis defines as "prayer first, music second."[7] Its very simplicity is intentional, as it is meant to aid the congregation in prayer and devotion rather than to create a sense of awe at its beauty and musicality. In these distinctions we start to see just how Gregorian chant has influenced church music throughout the centuries and even today. Even those of us who don't hear Gregorian chant in our churches wish for the music in our service to be seen as "prayer first." Many modern churches also see music as an integral part of their service of liturgy. The idea behind Gregorian chant and the fact that it was considered a sacred part of the liturgy were important steps in the worship life of the church.

▶▶▶▶▶ GOING FORWARD

Have another person read this section.

Thanking is yet another way we grow closer to God. As Edward M. Bounds wrote in the Devotional Reading, thanksgiving is remembrance. It happens when we consciously give voice to the gratitude we have in our souls, for all God has done and continues to do for us and for those around us. We often think of offering thanks to God as something we do in our individual and collective prayer time and as an important aspect of our worship, but it is also intricately woven into the sacrament of Eucharist, Communion, the Lord's Supper, which Jesus taught us to share. As we eat of the bread and drink of the cup, we remember Jesus and the incredible redeeming sacrifice he made for us.

And as we thank God during Communion, during our private times of prayer and our public times of worship, as we read the Psalms, we learn too the value of thanking as a Spiritual Discipline. Just as in the last chapter we read that praise is the consummation of happiness and therefore is more for our benefit than God's, so too does thanking God for our many blessings help to make those ways in which we do not feel blessed recede into the background. Thanking God has a way of straightening out our priorities and helping us see our lives with clarity, with the eyes of Christ. It builds in us a humble spirit, filled with gratitude and overflowing with love, the very embodiment of Jesus Christ our master.

What lessons have you learned from thanking God?

REFLECTION QUESTION
Again, allow each member a few moments to answer this question.

This concludes our look at thanking. In the next chapter we will turn our attention to another avenue of prayer and worship—celebrating.

SJ After everyone has had a chance to respond, the leader reads this paragraph.

CLOSING PRAYER

Incline your ear, O LORD, and answer me,
    for I am poor and needy,
Preserve my life, for I am devoted to you;
    save your servant who trusts in you.
You are my God; be gracious to me, O Lord,
    for to you do I cry all day long.
Gladden the soul of your servant,
    for to you, O Lord, I lift up my soul.
For you, O Lord, are good and forgiving,
    abounding in steadfast love to all who call on you.
Give ear, O LORD, to my prayer;
    listen to my cry of supplication.
In the day of my trouble I call on you,
    for you will answer me.

For you are great and do wondrous things;
    you alone are God.
Teach me your way, O LORD,
    that I may walk in your truth. (PS 86:1–7, 10–11a)

SJ Allow some time for members to encourage one another to read the Devotional and Scripture Readings and do the exercise in the following chapter before the next meeting. Then invite the members to be silent for a few moments before leading them in reading the Closing Prayer aloud together.

SJ At the end of the Closing Prayer, the leader asks for a volunteer to lead the next meeting.

TAKING IT FURTHER

Try thanking God for some of the things in your life that you do not typically see as blessings—for example, a boss or co-worker who is difficult to like, a temper tantrum your child throws, a traffic jam that makes you late. How does thanking God for these things change your attitude about them?

ADDITIONAL EXERCISE

Bounds, Edward M. *The Essentials of Prayer*. Grand Rapids, MI: Christian Classics Ethereal Library, 2004. Available at www.ccel.org.

ADDITIONAL RESOURCES

Are you more comfortable thanking others or being thanked? How does it feel when someone thanks you or when you are obliged to thank someone? What insight does this give you about thanksgiving as a Spiritual Discipline?

How does sharing in Communion strengthen your ties to the church community?

What has been your understanding of the Eucharist and its role in your life? How does thinking of it as an opportunity to thank God change or enhance your understanding?

CELEBRATING

12

DEVOTIONAL READING

TONY CAMPOLO, *The Kingdom of God Is a Party*

Once a year, according to what Moses wrote in Deuteronomy 14, all the people of God were to bring one-tenth of all their earnings to the temple in Jerusalem. Imagine! One-tenth of Israel's GNP! And it was not to be used for mission work. It was not to be used for charity. It was not even to be used to build an education annex onto the temple. It was to be used on a gigantic party....

Everybody was invited to the party, from widows who hadn't had a fun night out for a year, to poor kids who couldn't have come up with ticket money to whatever was the ancient equivalent of Disneyland. Prostitutes and tax collectors were invited. So what if their reputations were questionable? When it's a really good party, you forget all that stuff. Everybody forgot their titles and credentials at this wonderful party. The rich danced with the poor. Management did a "bottoms-up" with labor. The sophisticated intelligentsia sang something like "Auld Lang Syne" with the school dropouts. It was crazy!

If you are wondering what all this partying was about, let me tell you. The party was, and is, about the Kingdom of God. It has been planned by God to be a foretaste of what He has in mind for all of us when His Kingdom comes on earth as it is in heaven. Life may be hard. It may be full of troubles. But in the midst of it all, God tells us to set aside a tithe—a full 10 percent of all that we have earned through our labors—and to throw a party which will remind us of what God has in store for us.

The Scriptures tell us to spend all of this money for partying because it is in partying that we know a little something about the kind of God we have. He is not some kind of transcendental Shylock demanding His pound of flesh; He is not some kind of deistic chairperson of the universe. Our

> ✍ It is helpful for everyone to read the Devotional and Scripture Readings and do the My Life with God Exercise before the meeting. Begin the meeting with silent prayer, then move directly to Reflecting on My Life With God below.

God is a party deity. He loves a party. If you don't believe me, then just pay attention to what His Son Jesus had to say about his Father's Kingdom.

> The kingdom of heaven is like unto a certain king, which made a marriage for his son, And sent forth his servants to call them that were bidden to the wedding: and they would not come. (Matt. 22:2–4)

> And he saith unto me, Write, Blessed are they which are called unto the marriage supper of the Lamb. And he saith unto me, These are the true sayings of God. (Rev. 19:9)

Did you get that? Jesus says the Kingdom is like a wedding reception and He wants His friends to celebrate with Him as though He were the bridegroom. . . .

Just the other day, I preached this good news about the Kingdom of God and a young couple "got me" as soon as I had finished. They let it be known in no uncertain terms that they found my message objectionable. They claimed that the Kingdom of God was marked by pain, suffering, and sacrifice, and that I was distorting the biblical message to say otherwise.

Of course I disagreed. This is not to say that Christians do not have to endure pain, suffering, and sacrifice. The history of Christianity makes clear that the saints of the church have had to endure all of these things. Christians follow a Christ who was a Man of sorrows, well acquainted with grief. Jesus carried a cross, and He warned all those who would dare to follow Him that they would have to do the same. But the reason our Lord and those who become His followers endure all this grief is to create the Kingdom. The pain, the suffering, the sacrifice are all means to an end. And that end is the Kingdom of God.[1]

MY LIFE WITH GOD EXERCISE

The fact that the Mosaic law made provisions for the Israelites to *eat* their yearly tithe of grain and animals or, if something prevented them from going to Jerusalem, sell it and spend the money on whatever they desired—oxen, sheep, wine, strong drink—and throw a party amazes most people not familiar with the Old Testament (see Deut 14:22–27). Even those of us who have grown up in churches and belonged to Christian communities for a long time can find it hard to believe. Why? What kind of image do we have of God? A sourpuss who delights in making our life miserable by demanding that we give 10 percent of what we produce or earn to him? Or maybe a God who always has his hand out, demanding more, more, more? Or is it because that's the image we have of the Church—never satisfied with its income, always asking us for additional money?

At one time or another many of us have had at least one of these mental pictures of God and the Church. It can be hard to accept that God wants us to be happy, much less to celebrate. But take a look at the life of Jesus. He attended one of the most celebratory events in the life of Galilee villages: a wedding. Everyone was having such a good time that the supply of wine ran out. So what did he do? He made more! And Jesus's wine was even better than what the host had originally provided (John 2:1–10). The Gospels are full of accounts of people hosting Jesus at their houses for dinner—Martha, Zacchaeus, Simon the leper—dinners that included all types of people, especially those considered unblessable in Jesus's culture, like prostitutes, the disabled, tax collectors, and the nonreligious. He had such a good time at parties that people called him a glutton and "winebibber" (Luke 7:34, KJV). Jesus spoke of the celebratory nature of the kingdom. At the end of the parable of the lost coin, Jesus said, "There is joy in the presence of the angels of God over one sinner who repents" (Luke 15:10). Even the apostle Paul, whom many consider the penultimate sourpuss because of his stands on issues of personal morality, tells us, "Rejoice in the Lord always; again I will say, Rejoice" (Phil 4:4). Right before the passage from Revelation quoted by Tony Campolo in the Devotional Reading, there is rejoicing in heaven by a great multitude. Hallelujahs ring out. Praises go up. Exultations spread. And a marriage feast is prepared (19:1–8).

So where did we get this idea that it was improper to have a party in the kingdom of God? Probably from people who were trying to impose *their* ideas of proper decorum upon others. For much too long Christianity has been a sour-faced faith. So, here is what we would like to suggest that you do sometime during the next few days: throw a party! You can decide what kind of party you want to have—dinner, birthday, brunch, anniversary, patriotic, patio, costume, block, holiday, Super Bowl. Perhaps someone around you has achieved something that you can celebrate. Invite your friend. Invite your neighbor. Invite someone you would like to get acquainted with. Invite someone you know who lives alone. Invite a young person. Invite a person who may not have a good reputation. Invite an older person. Invite your pastor. Play games. Visit. Get acquainted. If you have to use some of the money that you planned to give to your church, do so. In the midst of the party, while everyone is having a good time, keep in mind your reason for having the party: that you are living out the joy you find in the kingdom of God. Think about the celebrating you are doing, and the diverse group of people with whom you are celebrating, as a small taste of the kingdom of God. Perhaps you might want to share this insight with one or more guests at the party, but be careful about alienating someone who may have had a bad experience with evangelism. Joy and a welcoming spirit can also be powerful witnesses.

REFLECTING ON MY LIFE WITH GOD
Allow each member a few moments to answer this question.

What happened at your party? If you haven't had a chance to have your party, what do you plan to do?

➤ SCRIPTURE READING: PSALM 84

✍ After everyone has had a chance to respond to the question, ask a member to read this passage from Scripture.

How lovely is your dwelling place,
    O LORD of hosts!
My soul longs, indeed it faints
    for the courts of the LORD;
my heart and my flesh sing for joy
    to the living God.

Even the sparrow finds a home,
    and the swallow a nest for herself,
    where she may lay her young,
at your altars, O LORD of hosts,
    my King and my God.
Happy are those who live in your house,
    ever singing your praise. *Selah.*

Happy are those whose strength is in you,
    in whose heart are the highways to Zion.
As they go through the valley of Baca
    they make it a place of springs;
    the early rain also covers it with pools.
They go from strength to strength;
    the God of gods will be seen in Zion.

O LORD God of hosts, hear my prayer;
    give ear, O God of Jacob!
Behold our shield, O God;
    look on the face of your anointed.

For a day in your courts is better
　　than a thousand elsewhere.
I would rather be a doorkeeper in the house of my God
　　than live in the tents of wickedness.
For the LORD God is a sun and shield;
　　he bestows favor and honor.
No good thing does the LORD withhold
　　from those who walk uprightly.
O LORD of hosts,
　　happy is everyone who trusts in you.

How do you feel after reading the Scripture?

REFLECTION QUESTION
Allow each person a few
moments to respond to
this question.

▶▶ GETTING THE PICTURE

Along with Psalm 130, which we studied in Chapter 7, Psalm 84 is one of the songs sung by pilgrims on the way to the Temple in Jerusalem. It is also sometimes called a Song of Zion for the same reason; the term *Zion* referred to Jerusalem and the Temple. Since the Temple both symbolized God's presence with his people Israel and was believed literally to be the place where God was present with his people, worship at the Temple was of great significance to the community.[2] Faithful Israelites made the trip to the Temple three times a year, for the feasts of Passover, Pentecost, and Tabernacles.[3] Other circumstances also called for special visits to the Temple. For example, Joseph and Mary made the trek to the Temple to present baby Jesus to the Lord, as was the custom for firstborn males (Luke 2:22–23). Jesus and his family also went to the Temple each year for Passover (2:41).

✍ After a brief discussion, choose one person to read this section.

As the pilgrims travel, they anticipate the joy of worshiping again in God's house: "My soul longs, indeed it faints for the courts of the LORD" (v 2). Just as the swallows and sparrows long for a secure home in which they and their offspring are safe, so too did the pilgrims anticipate the joy and security of the Lord's home. But the journey itself is also cause for celebration. Those who travel to Zion have their path blessed with abundant water: "They go from strength to strength" (v 7). It is also clear that the path to Zion is not just the physical road up to Jerusalem but also the path of our lives toward God. The psalmist writes of this joy of the journey in both a physical and emotional sense: "Happy are those . . . in

Celebrating

whose heart are the highways to Zion" (v 5). No matter whether they are physically in it or not, the fact that they have a true home, a home that is the Lord's, is something to celebrate. The psalmist and the pilgrims who sing his song recognize that their true home is not on this earth; it is with God: "A day in your courts is better than a thousand elsewhere" (v 10).

▶▶▶ GOING DEEPER

✍ Have another member read this section.

As the joyful tone of the psalm makes clear, all worship is at its heart celebration. Worship is celebrating God for who he is and what he does for us. God's goodness to us and his actions on our behalf are always cause for celebration. Celebration helps us put things into perspective. There was no mention of sufferings or needs by those who were traveling to the Temple; they knew that any of their problems were as nothing compared to the joy they would experience as they worshiped God in his Temple. So it is for us. All of the minor irritations and major disasters in our lives come into focus as we worship God for who he is: Father, Son, Holy Spirit; Creator, Redeemer, Sustainer; "I am that I am," Adonijah, Elohim; Prophet, Priest, King; Advocate, Comforter, Counselor. We also celebrate God's actions on our behalf. From his actions in history, including the unimaginable blessing of salvation through Jesus, to the blessings each of us has in our lives—how many times do we know that God has acted on our behalf and we have failed to acknowledge it, much less celebrated?

Reflecting on the true nature of God cannot help but bring us joy. The joy expressed in this psalm is not temporary happiness but a feeling of security, of well-being, of being comfortable in our own skin. It is the knowledge that God loves us for who we are and will work with us until we become who he created us to be. This joy is a fruit of the Spirit (Gal 5:22). It is the joy that erupts in laughter and mirth and finds pleasure in the small and the insignificant. This joy comes from within and does not depend on others to make us happy. It is settled; it is serene. This joy gives us strength.

Celebration also promotes community. There were not separate Temple times for rich and poor, man and woman, those who were descended from the tribe of Benjamin and those of the tribe of Judah. Everyone traveled to the Temple at the same feast times to celebrate and praise God together. During celebration, differences fade and we get to know better our neighbor, our family, our small group members, our co-workers. And when we know them better, we can love them. And when we love them, we come closer to fulfilling the command of Jesus to "love your neighbor as yourself" (Matt 22:39b).

Finally, Psalm 84 speaks to us because we are all journeying toward God. All of us who have a relationship with God hold in our hearts the pathway to Zion. The very journey toward God, the knowledge that we have a true home in the Lord, is something to celebrate. Just as the pilgrims celebrated with songs of praise before they reached the Temple, we too can celebrate God's kingdom even though we have yet to see it in its fullness. Just a glimpse is cause enough.

How has celebration been a part of your journey with God?

REFLECTION QUESTION
Allow each person a few moments to respond.

▶▶▶▶ POINTING TO GOD

The medieval German abbess Hildegard of Bingen is known for her writings, her skill as an administrator of convents, her healing gifts, and also her music. Her accomplishments are all the more remarkable when viewed in the near-complete dearth of similar accomplishments by any other twelfth-century woman. Her music in particular has recently come to greater notice, most notably her cycle of more than seventy songs and the musical "Play of the Virtues," which many consider the first musical drama. Together her chants and the musical comprise "The Symphony of the Harmony of the Heavenly Revelations." The title signifies Hildegard's belief that her music was inspired by God and that music was the highest form of praise to God. As Nancy Fierro writes,

✍ Choose one member to read this section.

> [Hildegard] believed that many times a day, we fall out of sorts, lose our way or find ourselves off center. Music was the sacred technology which could best tune humanity, redirect our hearts toward heaven and put our feet back onto the wholesome ways of God. 'Symphonia' was a key concept in Hildegard's thought and meant not only the joyful harmony achieved in blending voices and instruments but the spiritual field of unity we all long for when we sing. In singing and playing music, we integrate mind, heart and body, heal discord between us, and celebrate heavenly harmony here on earth. According to Hildegard, this becomes our 'opus'—the epitome of good work in the service of God.[4]

Celebrating

Hildegard had been a member of a religious order since she was a young girl, so she was greatly influenced by the Divine Office, a series of liturgical prayers consisting of eight one-hour sessions that served as the center of convent life. Most of the songs Hildegard composed during her lifetime were liturgical songs for the Divine Office, mostly in the Gregorian plainchant or plainsong style. But the joy and celebration inherent in her compositions set them apart. Fierro adds, "Unlike the mild, mainstream music of her day, [Hildegard's] lyrical speech breaks into rhapsodic emotion; her zesty melodies soar up to two and one half octaves, leaping and swirling into flourishing roulades which leave the singer breathless."[5] Just reading the lyrics of one of the antiphons (liturgical songs) she composed, about the relationship between God and his creation, one can feel her sense of joy and celebration:

> O how wonderful is the prescience of the divine heart,
> who foreknew every creature.
> For when God looked on the face of man,
> whom He had made,
> all his works
> He saw completed in his form.
> O how wonderful is the breath
> which brought man to life.[6]

The joyful leaps and expressive lyrics of Hildegard's music left a lasting impression on all those who heard them. Like the psalm we read in the Scripture Reading, her liturgical songs encouraged her listeners to celebrate God and our own journey toward communion with him.

▶▶▶▶▶ GOING FORWARD

Have another person read this section.

In *Celebration of Discipline* Richard Foster makes the statement, "Celebration is at the heart of the way of Christ."[7] He then explains that Jesus's birth was announced with joy by the angels and that Jesus bequeathed his joy to the disciples the night before his death: "I have said these things to you so that my joy may be in you, and that your joy may be complete" (John 15:11). Remember Jesus said this while he and his disciples were observing Passover, the feast during which they remembered and celebrated their ancestors' delivery from slavery. He knew that "celebration brings joy into life, and joy makes us strong."[8] Celebrating Passover with his followers helped give Jesus the strength to face down and conquer death. Jesus knew that the pain, sacrifice, and sufferings that we as humans endure on this earth are only temporary and will seem as nothing compared with the eternal glory of the kingdom of God. Our eternity is not about sacrifice; it is about our future celebrating with God in his kingdom.

How have times of celebration strengthened you for times of trial?

REFLECTION QUESTION
Again, allow each member a few moments to answer this question.

CLOSING PRAYER

Incline your ear, O LORD, and answer me,
    for I am poor and needy,
Preserve my life, for I am devoted to you;
    save your servant who trusts in you.
You are my God; be gracious to me, O Lord,
    for to you do I cry all day long.
Gladden the soul of your servant,
    for to you, O Lord, I lift up my soul.
For you, O Lord, are good and forgiving,
    abounding in steadfast love to all who call on you.
Give ear, O LORD, to my prayer;
    listen to my cry of supplication.
In the day of my trouble I call on you,
    for you will answer me.

For you are great and do wondrous things;
    you alone are God.
Teach me your way, O LORD,
    that I may walk in your truth. (PS 86:1–7, 10–11a)

↪ After everyone has had a chance to respond, remind them that this is the last lesson in the book and ask the group if they would like to continue meeting. If everyone agrees to continue, this would be a good time to discuss when to meet and what material to use. When everyone has shared, the leader asks the members to be silent for a few moments before leading them in reading the Closing Prayer aloud together.

TAKING IT FURTHER

ADDITIONAL EXERCISE

The next time you feel off-kilter or disconnected from God, follow Hildegard of Bingen's counsel and try singing one of your favorite hymns or praise songs, playing your instrument, or listening to an uplifting and meaningful piece of music. Does it help restore you to God? Does it create in you a sense of joy and celebration at the wonderful promise of the kingdom of God?

Celebrating

ADDITIONAL RESOURCES

Campolo, Tony. *The Kingdom of God Is a Party*. Dallas, TX: Word, 1990.

Flanagan, Sabina. *Hildegard of Bingen: A Visionary Life*. New York: Routledge, 1988.

Foster, Richard J. *Celebration of Discipline*. San Francisco: HarperSan-Francisco, 1998.

ADDITIONAL REFLECTION QUESTIONS

Why do you think the Church has traditionally been viewed as sour-faced? How well does your church do at demonstrating the celebratory nature of God's kingdom? How could you improve?

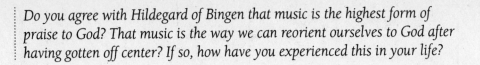

Do you agree with Hildegard of Bingen that music is the highest form of praise to God? That music is the way we can reorient ourselves to God after having gotten off center? If so, how have you experienced this in your life?

Do you tend to feel more connected to God, more aware of him, during times of celebration or times of trouble? Why?

NOTES

CHAPTER 1: LONGING

1. Os Guinness, *Long Journey Home* (Colorado Springs, CO: Waterbrook, 2001), 1–2, 191.
2. John of the Cross, *Living Flame of Love: Stanza 3,* cited in David Hazard, *You Set My Spirit Free* (Minneapolis, MN: Bethany, 1994), 26–28.
3. Janet Lindeblad Janzen with Richard J. Foster, *Songs for Renewal* (San Francisco: HarperSanFrancisco, 1995), 20.
4. John Wimber, *Worship: Intimacy with God,* available at http://www.crvineyard.org/Wimber/WIMBER5.htm.
5. A. W. Tozer, *The Pursuit of God* (Harrisburg, PA: Christian Publications, 1982), 15, 17.

CHAPTER 2: EXHORTING

1. Martin Luther, *Luther's Works,* vol. 43, ed. Gustav Wiencke (Minneapolis, MN: Augsburg Fortress, 1968), cited in Archie Parrish, *A Simple Way to Pray* (Marietta, GA: Serve International, 2005), 36–39.
2. Dallas Willard, *The Divine Conspiracy* (San Francisco: HarperSanFrancisco, 1998), 274.
3. Evelyn Underhill, *Essential Writings,* ed. Emilie Griffin (Maryknoll, NY: Orbis, 2003), 129–30.

CHAPTER 3: REPENTING

1. Eugene H. Peterson, *A Long Obedience in the Same Direction* (Downers Grove, IL: InterVarsity, 2000), 29–31.
2. Richard J. Foster and others, eds., *The Renovaré Spiritual Formation Bible* (San Francisco: HarperSanFrancisco, 2005), 820.
3. A. A. Anderson, *Psalms: The New Century Bible Commentary,* vol. 1 (Grand Rapids, MI: Eerdmans, 1972), 392.
4. Available at http://www.nyise.org/fanny/songbird2.html.
5. Jack Schrader, ed., *Sing Joyfully* (Carol Stream, IL: Hope Tabernacle, 1989), 366.

CHAPTER 4: ASKING

1. Agnes Sanford, *The Healing Light* (Plainfield, NJ: Logos International, 1972), 1–3.
2. Richard J. Foster, *Celebration of Discipline* (San Francisco: HarperSanFrancisco, 1998), 40.
3. Foster, *Celebration of Discipline,* 37.
4. *John and Charles Wesley: Selected Prayers, Hymns, and Sermons* (San Francisco: HarperSanFrancisco, 1981), 79–81.
5. Foster, *Celebration of Discipline,* 39.

CHAPTER 5: PLEADING

1. Alexander Whyte, *Lord Teach Us to Pray* (London: Hodder & Stoughton, 1922), 79–80, available at www.ccel.org.
2. Thomas Dorsey, "Take My Hand, Precious Lord," *Old Fashioned Revival Hour Songs* (Winona Lake, IN: Rodeheaver, Hall-Mack, 1950), 79.

CHAPTER 6: CURSING

1. Kathleen Norris, *Amazing Grace* (New York: Riverhead, 1998), 69–70.
2. Sigmund Mowinckel, *The Psalms in Israel's Worship* (Grand Rapids, MI: Eerdmans, 2004), 48–49.
3. Mowinckel, *The Psalms in Israel's Worship,* 49.
4. Bernhard W. Anderson, *Out of the Depths: The Psalms Speak for Us Today* (Philadelphia: Westminster, 1970), 60.
5. Eugene H. Peterson, *Answering God: The Psalms as Tools for Prayer* (San Francisco: HarperSanFrancisco, 1989), 98.
6. Peterson, *Answering God,* 99.

CHAPTER 7: WAITING

1. Luci Shaw, *Water My Soul* (Grand Rapids, MI: Zondervan, 1998), 83–86.
2. Paul J. Achtemeier, ed., *Harper's Bible Dictionary* (San Francisco: HarperSanFrancisco, 1985), 686.
3. Peterson, *A Long Obedience in the Same Direction,* 144.
4. Philip Yancey, "God Behind Barbed Wire," *Christianity Today* (Sept. 2005), 120.
5. Yancey, "God Behind Barbed Wire," 120.
6. Willard, *The Divine Conspiracy,* 89.
7. David Schrader, "Song Story: Matt Redman's 'The Heart of Worship,'" available at http://www.crosswalk.com/faith/worship_center/1253122.html.
8. Schrader, "Song Story."

CHAPTER 8: LAMENTING

1. Nicholas Wolterstorff, *Lament for a Son* (Grand Rapids, MI: Eerdmans, 1987), 52–58.
2. Anderson, *Psalms,* 186.
3. W. H. Bellinger Jr., *Psalms: Reading and Studying the Book of Praises* (Peabody, MA: Hendrickson, 1990), 57.
4. Cited in Kevin Twit, "Anne Steele," available at http://www.igracemusic.com/hymnbook/authors/anne_steele.html.
5. Available at http://www.igracemusic.com/hymnbook/authors/anne_steele.html.
6. Bellinger, *Psalms,* 72.

CHAPTER 9: TRUSTING

1. Paul Gerhardt, "Christian Trust," in *Religious Poems,* trans. John Wesley (New York: Thomas Y. Crowell, n.d.), 380–81.
2. Eugene H. Peterson, *Leap Over a Wall: Earthy Spirituality for Everyday Christians* (San Francisco: HarperSanFrancisco, 1997), 16.
3. Frank E. Gaebelein, ed., *The Expositor's Bible Commentary,* vol. 5 (Grand Rapids, MI: Zondervan, 1991), 298.
4. "A Sacrifice of Praise," *Charisma* (Jan. 2006), available at http://www.charismamag.com/display.php?id=12185.
5. Jack Schrader, ed., *Sing Joyfully* (Carol Stream, IL: Tabernacle, 1989), Hymn 450.

CHAPTER 10: PRAISING

1. Thomas Merton, *Praying the Psalms* (Collegeville, MN: Liturgical, 1956), 10–12.
2. C. S. Lewis, *Reflections on the Psalms* (New York: Harvest/Harcourt Brace Jovanovich, 1958), 90.
3. Lewis, *Reflections,* 94, 95.
4. "Praise God from Whom All Blessings Flow," *Favorite Hymns of Praise* (Chicago, IL: Tabernacle/Standard, 1968).

5. See http://www.biblepicturegallery.com/pictures/L-Music.htm for pictures of instruments used during biblical times.
6. Merton, *Praying the Psalms*, 13.
7. Henley Denmead, "Messiah by George Frideric Handel," available at http://www.hartfordchorale.org/Messiah.htm.
8. David Vickers, *Messiah: A Sacred Oratorio*, available at http://www.ghandel.org.
9. "On the Authority of the Earl of Kinnoul," *Biographica Dramatica*, cited in G. Hogarth: *Musical History, Biography and Criticism* (1838) and James Beattie (1780), available at http://www.gfhandel.org.
10. Denmead, "Messiah."
11. Vickers, *Messiah*.
12. *Messiah: Libretto*, available at http://www.gfhandel.org.

CHAPTER 11: THANKING

1. Edward M. Bounds, *The Essentials of Prayer* (Grand Rapids MI: Christian Classics Ethereal Library, 2004), 14–15, available at www.ccel.org.
2. Achtemeier, ed., *Harper's Bible Dictionary*, 754.
3. Achtemeier, ed., *Harper's Bible Dictionary*, 577.
4. Foster and others, eds., *The Renovaré Spiritual Formation Bible*, 1.
5. Angelo De Santi, "Liturgical Chant," in *The Catholic Encyclopedia*, vol. 9 (2003), available at http://www.newadvent.org/cathen/09304a.htm.
6. Stephen Thuis, "Gregorian Chant: A Barometer of Religious Fervor," available at http://www.unavoce.org/chantbar.htm.
7. Thuis, "Gregorian Chant."

CHAPTER 12: CELEBRATING

1. Tony Campolo, *The Kingdom of God Is a Party* (Dallas, TX: Word, 1990), 25–29.
2. Bellinger, *Psalms*, 23, 158.
3. Peterson, *A Long Obedience in the Same Direction*, 18.
4. Nancy Fierro, *Hildegard of Bingen: Symphony of the Harmony of Heaven*, available at http://www.staff.uni-mainz.de/horst/hildegard/music/music.html.
5. Fierro, *Hildegard of Bingen*.
6. Sabina Flanagan, *Hildegard of Bingen: A Visionary Life* (New York: Routledge, 1988), 107.
7. Foster, *Celebration of Discipline*, 190.
8. Foster, *Celebration of Discipline*, 191.

ABOUT THE AUTHORS

Richard J. Foster is the founder of RENOVARÉ; author of six books, including *Celebration of Discipline, PRAYER: Finding the Heart's True Home,* and *Streams of Living Water;* and Editor of *The Renovaré Spiritual Formation Bible,* all of which effectively promote personal spiritual renewal. From his base near Denver, Colorado, Richard travels throughout the world, speaking and teaching on the spiritual life.

Lynda L. Graybeal has worked as Richard Foster's personal assistant for over two decades and was the Administrator/Editor of RENOVARÉ until 2004. She has written articles for the *RENOVARÉ Perspective* and appendices in *Streams of Living Water,* and was a General Editor of *The Renovaré Spiritual Formation Bible.* She lives in Canyon, Texas.

Julia L. Roller is a freelance writer and editor, was the project editor for *The Renovaré Spiritual Formation Bible,* and has written for publications such as *Group Magazine, Rev!, Children's Ministry, Go Deeper Retreats,* and *Young Adult Ministry in the 21st Century.* She lives in Coronado, California.

ACKNOWLEDGMENTS

The seeds of this book lie in the rich material found in *The Renovaré Spiritual Formation Bible*, so first we must acknowledge and thank the other editors of that project—Richard J. Foster, Gayle Beebe, Thomas C. Oden, and Dallas Willard. Lyle SmithGraybeal has greatly enriched this guide with both his enthusiastic wellspring of ideas and his patient editing. At HarperOne Cynthia DiTiberio has also done a wonderful job with the editing of the manuscript. Michael G. Maudlin of HarperOne, Richard J. Foster and Lyle SmithGraybeal from Renovaré, and Kathryn Helmers of Helmers Literary Services first envisioned this series of spiritual formation guides, so we thank them for their support and encouragement as well as for the faith they had in us. Finally, we are especially grateful to our families, particularly our spouses, Phil Graybeal and Ryan Waterman, for their support, inspiration, and love.

Lynda L. Graybeal and Julia L. Roller

Grateful acknowledgment is made to the following for permission to reprint material copyrighted or controlled by them.

The Scripture quotations contained herein are from the *New Revised Standard Version Bible*. Copyright © 1989, 1993, by the Division of Christian Education of the National Council of the Churches of Christ in the United States of America. Used by permission. All rights reserved.

Excerpts from and adaptation of "The With-God Life: A General Introduction" from *The Renovaré Spiritual Formation Bible* by Renovaré and edited by Richard J. Foster. Copyright © 2005 by Renovaré, Inc. Used with permission of HarperCollins Publishers, 10 East 53rd Street, New York, NY, 10022-5299, www.harpercollins.com.

PRAYER AND WORSHIP

WHAT IS Renovaré?

Renovaré (from the Latin meaning "to renew") is an infrachurch movement committed to the renewal of the Church of Jesus Christ in all its multifaceted expressions. Founded by best-selling author Richard J. Foster, Renovaré is Christian in commitment, international in scope, and ecumenical in breadth.

In *The Renovaré Spiritual Formation Bible,* we observe how God spiritually formed his people through historical events and the practice of Spiritual Disciplines that is The With-God Life. Renovaré continues this emphasis on spiritual formation by placing it within the context of the two-thousand-year history of the Church and six great Christian traditions we find in its life—Contemplative: The Prayer-Filled Life; Holiness: The Virtuous Life; Charismatic: The Spirit-Empowered Life; Social Justice: The Compassionate Life; Evangelical: The Word-Centered Life; and Incarnational: The Sacramental Life. This balanced vision of Christian faith and witness was modeled for us by Jesus Christ and was evident in the lives of countless saints: Antony, Francis of Assisi, Susanna Wesley, Phoebe Palmer, and others. The With-God Life of the People of God continues on today as Christians participate in the life and practices of local churches and look forward to spending eternity in that "all-inclusive community of loving persons with God himself at the very center of this community as its prime Sustainer and most glorious Inhabitant."

In addition to offering a balanced vision of the spiritual life, Renovaré promotes a practical strategy for people seeking renewal by helping facilitate small spiritual formation groups; national, regional, and local conferences; one-day seminars; personal and group retreats; and readings from devotional classics that can sustain a long-term commitment to renewal. Renovaré Resources for Spiritual Renewal, Spiritual Formation Guides, and *The Renovaré Spiritual Formation Bible*—books published by HarperSanFrancisco—seek to integrate historical, scholarly, and inspirational materials into practical, readable formats. These resources can be used in a variety of settings, including small groups, private and organizational retreats, individual devotions, and church school classes. Written and edited by people committed to the renewal of the Church, all of the materials present a balanced vision of Christian life and faith coupled with a practical strategy for spiritual growth and enrichment.

For more information about Renovaré and its mission, please log on to its Web site (www.renovare.org) or write Renovaré, 8 Inverness Drive East, Suite 102, Englewood, CO 80112-5624, USA.

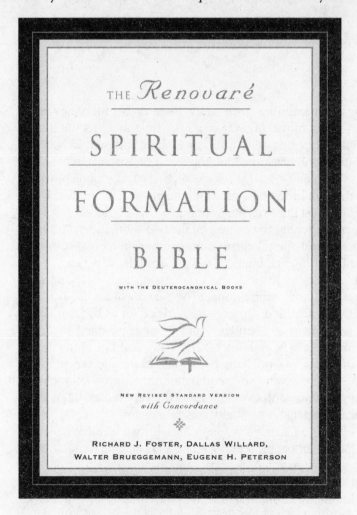